2020

ROMAN REPLIES

&

CLSA ADVISORY OPINIONS

DONNA MILLER, JD, JCL
EDITOR, ROMAN REPLIES

VERY REV. PATRICK COONEY, OSB, JCL
REV. MSGR. MICHAEL A. SOUCKAR, JCD
EDITORS, ADVISORY OPINIONS

Canon Law Society of America

ISBN 978-1-932208-56-6
ISSN 1543-4230
SAN 237-6296

The Canon Law Society of America's programs and publications are designed solely to help canonists maintain their professional competence. In dealing with specific canonical matters, the canonist using Canon Law Society of America (CLSA) publications or orally conveyed information should also research original sources of authority.

The views and opinions expressed in this publication are those of the individual authors and do not represent the views of the CLSA, its Board of Governors, staff or members. The CLSA does not endorse the views or opinions expressed by the individual authors. The publisher and authors specifically disclaim any liability, loss or risk, personal or otherwise, which is claimed as a consequence, directly or indirectly, of the use, reliance, or application of any of the contents of this publication.

Unless otherwise noted, all canons quoted are from the *Code of Canon Law, Latin-English Edition* (Washington, DC: Canon Law Society of America, 2020) and the *Code of Canons of the Eastern Churches, Latin-English Edition* (Washington, DC: Canon Law Society of America, 2002).

Printed in the United States of America.

Canon Law Society of America
415 Michigan Avenue NE, Suite 101
Washington, DC 20017-4502

TABLE OF CONTENTS

Foreword..7

ROMAN REPLIES 2020

Introductory Note..11

CANONS 127, 166, 627, AND 631: Regarding the Use
of Telecommunications for Sharing between Members
of Institutes and Societies..13

CANONS 127 AND 166: Regarding the Use of Telecommunications
for the Convocation of Various Ecclesiastical Structures 16

CANONS 631-633: Postponement of General and
Provincial Chapters 18

CANON 694 §1, 3°: Regarding the Application of *Ipso Facto*
Dismissal of a Religious for Illegitimate Absence 19

CANON 850; *RITUALE ROMANO*: The Validity of Baptisms
Administered with Words Other Than Those Prescribed
in the Approved Liturgical Books in Cases That Do Not
Involve Urgent Necessity 28

CANONS 976 AND 986 §2: Right of Accused Cleric to
Petition for Dispensation from Clerical Obligations 37

CANONS 1308-1310: Pious Foundations 40

CANON 880 §1: Use of Instruments for Administering
Confirmation During a Pandemic...41

CANONS 1478, 1481, 1505, 1508, AND 1545, AND
DIGNITAS CONNUBII 97, 101, AND 127:
Regarding Citation of a Violent Respondent............................42

CANON 1548 and VOS ESTIS LUX MUNDI:
Reporting Accusations and Privacy Issues.................................45

OTHER VATICAN DOCUMENTS

APOSTOLIC LETTER ISSUED *MOTU PROPRIO* FOR THE
CHANGE OF THE NAME OF THE VATICAN SECRET
ARCHIVE TO THE VATICAN APOSTOLIC ARCHIVE........................49

APOSTOLIC LETTER ISSUED *MOTU PROPRIO* BY THE
SUPREME PONTIFF FRANCIS REGARDING THE OFFICE
OF DEAN OF THE COLLEGE OF CARDINALS....................................52

CONGREGATION FOR THE DOCTRINE OF THE FAITH
RESCRIPTUM EX AUDIENTIA SS.MI...54

SECRETARY OF STATE
RESCRIPTUM EX AUDIENTIA SS.MI...55

ADDRESS OF HIS HOLINESS POPE FRANCIS TO PARTICIPANTS
IN THE PLENARY ASSEMBLY OF THE PONTIFICAL
COUNCIL FOR LEGISLATIVE TEXTS...56

ADDRESS OF HIS HOLINESS POPE FRANCIS TO THE
OFFICIALS OF THE TRIBUNAL OF THE ROMAN ROTA
FOR THE INAUGURATION OF THE JUDICIAL YEAR 59

NOTE FROM THE APOSTOLIC PENITENTIARY ON THE
SACRAMENT OF RECONCILIATION IN THE
CURRENT PANDEMIC 64

CONGREGATION FOR CLERGY ON ALIENATION
AND BANKRUPTCY PROCEEDINGS..66

CONGREGATION FOR THE DOCTRINE OF THE FAITH
VADEMECUM ON CERTAIN POINTS OF PROCEDURE
IN TREATING CASES OF SEXUAL ABUSE OF MINORS
COMMITTED BY CLERICS...67

ADVISORY OPINIONS 2020

Introductory Note...101

CIC CANON 285, §1 and §2; CCEO CANON 382: On the Carrying
of a Firearm by a Priest in Church as a Protective Measure....................103

CANON 291 AND THE 1980 NORMAE PROCEDURALES, ART. 4:
Suspensio ad Cautelam for Priests Requesting "Laicization"..................105

CANON 294: Ecclesiastical Circumscriptions and Their
    Relationship with the Diocesan Bishop...110

CANON 603: Transfer of a Diocesan Hermit or Hermitess 114

CANON 636: Finance Officer in a Religious Institute....................................118

CANON 668: Relatives Raising Questions Regarding a
    Sister's Inheritance...120

CIC 822, 212§3; CCEO 651, 15§3: When Clerics and Bishops
    Clash over What Constitutes Appropriate Use of Social Media 123

CANONS 843 §1; 213: The Right to the Sacraments
    During a Pandemic...131

CANON 1247: Whether a Vigil Mass Can Fulfill Two Obligations................143

CANON 1263: Diocesan Taxes...146

CANON 1447 AND DIGNITAS CONNUBII ART. 36 AND 66:
    From Judge to Defender of the Bond in the Same Cause?......................150

CANONS 1483, 1484: Whether the Ex Officio Appointment of a
    Procurator-Advocate Is Subject to Diocesan Limitations?......................153

CANON 1673 §§ 3 AND 4: Whether a Judicial Vicar Can Appoint a
    Sole Judge in Cases of Nullity of Marriage..156

SST ARTICLE 6, §1, 2°: Temporary Possession in Penal Law......................160

Contributors 163

FOREWORD

The Canon Law Society of America (CLSA) publishes annually *Roman Replies and CLSA Advisory Opinions* for canonists and those seeking a clearer understanding of the *praxis legis* of the Catholic Church. The combination of these two services, begun in 1984, continues to serve as useful resources for those involved in the application of canonical discipline.

The compilation of materials for *Roman Replies 2020* was guided by Donna Miller, Executive Coordinator of the CLSA and a member of the CLSA Publications Advisory Board. The collection of entries in this issue, when viewed in conjunction with previous volumes, assists the reader both in understanding recent developments in the law and in identifying current trends in the praxis of the Roman Curia.

The selection, editing, and assembly of opinions for *CLSA Advisory Opinions 2020* were provided by Reverend Patrick Cooney, OSB, and Monsignor Michael A. Souckar. The topics addressed in the opinions reflect a variety of canonical issues and demonstrate the scope of canonical expertise and reflection by members of the Society. Editorial assistance was provided by the CLSA Executive Coordinator.

Roman Replies and CLSA Advisory Opinions that are out-of-print are available electronically on the CLSA website (www.clsa.org).

The CLSA provides this series as a professional resource. Care should be taken in considering the relative weight of the materials found in this publication. The principles for canonical interpretation (*CIC* cc. 16-19 and *CCEO* cc. 1498-1501) serve as guides in considering the contents of this volume.

ROMAN REPLIES

INTRODUCTORY NOTE

The following is the editorial policy of Roman Replies. The policy, as well as the source of these materials, was first described in the 1984 edition and, with some modifications, has been in effect since that time.

Each year members of the Canon Law Society of America are invited to submit recent replies from the various dicasteries of the Holy See which might be of interest to the Society's members and the wider church. Judicial vicars, chancellors, vicars general, major superiors of institutes of consecrated life and societies of apostolic life in the United States, and professors of canon law are encouraged and asked to submit material for this important publication.

Contributions from members of the Society resident in other countries or members of other canon law societies are always most welcome. All contributors receive a complimentary copy of the volume.

Certain editorial principles determine the selection of documents for this publication. First, in general, entries which have already appeared in various canonical journals would not normally be repeated here. An exception is the publication of an official English translation of documents for which an unofficial translation already has been published. Second, documents which merely restate something published earlier with no added nuances or changes are not normally included. Third, documents that concern a matter not yet resolved by the Roman dicasteries are held for future publication in the hope that the entire matter may be fully reported when the question or controversy has been resolved. Finally, all details of names and places are changed to protect confidentiality, unless otherwise specified by the submitting individual.

A special note of thanks to all those who have submitted texts, helped with translations and who otherwise contributed to this 2020 edition. It is our hope that this volume continues to be a service to all who work in the ministry of justice in the Church.

Contributions may be sent to:

Canon Law Society of America
415 Michigan Avenue NE, Suite 101
Washington, DC 20017-4502

CANONS 127, 166, 627, AND 631

REGARDING THE USE OF TELECOMMUNICATIONS FOR SHARING BETWEEN MEMBERS OF INSTITUTES AND SOCIETIES

The Covid-19 global pandemic has drastically disrupted the ability of organizational leaders throughout the world to communicate through in-person gatherings. Superiors of religious institutes and societies of apostolic life, particularly those with international membership, sought an opinion on whether they could hold meetings through electronic means. The response of the Congregation for Institutes of Consecrated Life and Societies of Apostolic Life follows.

RESPONSE

Congregation for Institutes of Consecrated Life
and Societies of Apostolic Life

Prot. n. Sp.R. 2452/20
Vatican City, 1 July 2020

To General Moderators,

As a result of the COVID 19 pandemic, the Congregation for Institutes of Consecrated Life and Societies of Apostolic Life has received many requests for clarification regarding the possibility of using means of telecommunications for sharing between members of a "*coetus personarum*" ad *mentem* in the sense of can. 627 and with the inclusion of references to cann. 127 and 166. The same request was formulated by some Institutes and Societies in relation to General Chapters (cf. can. 631).

In order to contain the spread of this pandemic, national legislation has adopted restrictive measures regarding rail, air, sea and, in some cases even, road travel. In many cases, this has resulted in the impossibility of travel by members of the General / Provincial Councils or similar bodies. Councilors, being unable to comply with the *personal presence* as prescribed by can. 166§1, due to restrictions on movement, are prevented from offering their proper collaboration to the Major Superior.

1. The Holy Father, during the audience of June 30 of this year (Prot. n. Sp. R. 2452/20), has granted the Congregation for Institutes of Consecrated Life and Societies of Apostolic Life an "extraordinary faculty", approved in specific form which authorizes the Dicastery to dispense for individual cases, the physical presence of councilors according to the prescriptions of can. 166 §1. In this way,

the above mentioned difficulties which would have prevented the presence of the members of the Council at the meeting location are eliminated.

2. A meeting using telecommunications, of the Major Superior with his/her Council is not an ordinary solution for the governance of an Institute or a Province. In fact, once the state of emergency caused by the COVID 19 pandemic is resolved, *habitual* recourse to telecommunications would render meaningless the service of authority which, in consecrated life, calls for personally and responsibly maintaining a network of relationships through correct and effective communication in order to safeguard and promote communion in the Institute.

3. The Major Superior, when in the exercise of his/her office is obliged to make use of the work of the Council (cf. can. 627§1), will submit a request to the Congregation for Institutes of Consecrated Life and Societies of Apostolic Life to use telecommunications for a formal meeting with the Council. In this case, the minutes are drawn up as customary.

4. The Dicastery, having carefully considered the reasons for the requests already received, has decided upon the following:

> - that in the use of connection systems, confidentiality and, in the case of required secrecy, both must be ensured (cf. can. 127);
> - the identity of the participants in the telecommunication meeting must be verified;
> - the possibility of intervening in real time during the deliberations must be ensured.

The use of telecommunications is based on trust and calls for everyone's sense of responsibility so that technology can serve discernment and sound governance.

5. Synodality, in the particular or specific form of chapter collegiality, is at the heart of the work of renewal of the ICL-SAL promoted by the Second Vatican Council and indicates a specific *modus vivendi et operandi* of consecrated persons within the Church, the People of God. Synodality manifests and concretely realizes being in communion, in walking together, in coming together and in the active participation of all members in the evangelizing mission embodied by their own charism. The secular tradition of chapters calls for *physical presence* as a way of safeguarding and promoting the constant search for the common good. Physical presence combines the demands of representing the "entire institute [...] a true sign of its unity in charity" (can. 631§1). Physical presence is the expression of walking together in direct discussion, and communication, not only verbal, in taking on the challenge of different approaches and, if necessary, in more correctly reconsidering a *status quaestionis* before proceeding to definitive

resolutions that bind the whole Institute or Society. Physical presence involves the delicate and complex management of elective procedures and the election of Major Superiors: events and procedures that cannot be replaced even by the most sophisticated instruments of telecommunications.

6. In fact, the exercise of collegiality and collegial acts, by their very nature, cannot be reduced to the sum of the votes of the individual members of the chapter, since the synodal/collegial path itself is an integral part of the formation not only of a majority but, even more, of a consensus that arises from shared discernment. It is well known to all those who have experienced chapters that the formation of consensus is the result of direct *dialogue*, which, through physical presence, is assured with respect to timing and manner of communication. This would not seem as effective solely by means of telecommunications.

If for a *coetus personarum* (cf. above) an exception can be considered, its extension would lessen the significance of the exercise of collegiality by depriving it of its *added value*: the exercise of a process of discernment aimed at safeguarding the correctness of methods and the strict evaluation of decisions to promote the pursuit of the common good. A *purely* technical (virtual) collegiality risks weakening the sense of co-responsibility or, at least, weakening the conditions of an accurate assessment of its effectiveness.

7. On the occasion of the above mentioned audience granted to the Superiors of the Dicastery, the Holy Father decreed, accepting the request of the same Superiors, that no general or provincial chapters could be held by means of telecommunications, nor the combination of partial physical presence and partial presence through telecommunications, but only by means of physical presence.

As Pope Francis affirmed: "Clearly, it is not enough to multiply connections in order to increase mutual understanding". Even for us, as consecrated men and women, the Pope's question cannot be evaded: "How, then, can we find our true communitarian identity, aware of the responsibility we have towards one another in the online network as well?" (FRANCIS, *Message of the Holy Father Francis for the 53rd World Communications Day*, 24 January, 2019).

JOÁO BRAZ Card. de Aviz
Prefect

✠JOSÉ RODRÌGUEZ CARBALLO, O.F.M.
    Archbishop Secretary

Canons 127 and 166

Regarding the Use of Telecommunications for the Convocation of Various Ecclesiastical Structures

The Covid-19 global pandemic has drastically disrupted the ability of organizational leaders throughout the world to communicate through in-person gatherings. The United States Conference of Catholic Bishops sought an opinion on whether they could hold meetings through electronic means. The response of the Congregation for Clergy follows.

Congregation for Clergy

From the Vatican, 8 May 2020

Prot. N.

Your Excellency,

In response to your letter of 4 May last, wherein Your Excellency posed the question whether the convocations mentioned in *CIC* canon 127 and 166 may be carried out by technological means, the Congregation would offer the following animadversion.

The underlying *ratio legis* of the aforementioned canons would require that the meetings of the various councils take place by means of videoconference (e.g. methods such as Skype, Zoom, etc.) in such a way that those convoked might be effectively present contemporaneously-even in a virtual manner- to be consulted as a College or Council, whenever required by law. In written Minutes of such meetings, it will be necessary to make mention of the legitimate convocation of everyone who has a right to participate, as well as the particular virtual method through which the College or Council was consulted.

Finally, in addition to the points made above, I would like to clarify that—to guarantee the gathering of the College or Council and not merely the hearing of its members as individuals—consultation by individual telephone calls or emails to the persons who compose the interested diocesan College or Council must be avoided.

Under these same conditions, but only for so long as it remains a necessity (rebus sic stantibus), the convocations required by canons 127 and 166 may be conducted, by the virtual means favorably mentioned, in any ecclesiastical circumscription so affected. However, when possible, such consultations should be delayed until they may be carried out in the usual manner required by law.

With assurance of prayer for the Bishops and faithful of the United States, I am,

Sincerely yours in Christ,

✠Beniamino Cardinal Stella
Prefect

CANONS 631-633

POSTPONEMENT OF GENERAL AND PROVINCIAL CHAPTERS

In early 2020, superiors of religious institutes and societies of apostolic life inquired about the possibility of postponing their general chapters due to hardships caused by the Covid-19 pandemic.

RESPONSE

CONGREGATIO PRO INSTITUTIS VITAE CONSECRATAE ET SOCIETATIBUS VITAE APOSTOLICAE

Vatican City 2 April 2020
Prot. n.

In view of the measures being taken by governments and, in particular, the restrictions on movement and travel as a result of the pandemic emergency caused by Covid-19, the Congregation for Institutes of Consecrated Life and Societies of Apostolic Life provides the following:

- authorization for the postponement of the celebration of general and provincial chapters to a date to be determined;
- once the new dates for the celebration of the chapter have been established, the Dicastery should be informed by a written communication sent by e-mail to the following address segr@religiosi.va; or by fax to the following number: + 39 06 6988 4526;
- at the same time, it is to be noted that the mandates of the major superiors and their respective councils are extended until the next celebration of the chapters;
- these indications take effect from the date of issue of the General Decree CICLSAL Prot. No. Sp.R. 2419/20 of 2 April 2020 and will remain in force until new provisions are given.

JOÁO BRAZ Card. de Aviz
Prefect

✠JOSÉ RODRÌGUEZ CARBALLO, O.F.M.
Archbishop Secretary

CANON 694 §1, 3⁰

REGARDING THE APPLICATION OF *IPSO FACTO* DISMISSAL OF A RELIGIOUS FOR ILLEGITIMATE ABSENCE

In March of 2019, Pope Francis issued the apostolic letter motu proprio Communis vita, *which modified canon 694 by adding illegitimate absence for twelve consecutive months as a reason that religious must be held as* ipso facto *dismissed from the institute.[1] The English translation of the apostolic letter on the Vatican website raised questions for numerous superiors who were considering whether this provision was applicable to their members who were illegitimately absent for at least twelve consecutive months. The following inquiry was submitted to the Pontifical Council for Legislative Texts.*

INQUIRY

We have encountered conflicting interpretations of the application of *Communis vita* as it applies to canon 694, para. 1, no. 3. Does the twelve-month time frame for *ipso facto* dismissal apply only when a member of a religious institute is unable to be located? The Latin original reads: "prae oculis habita eiusdem sodalis irreperibilitate."[2] The English translation of the Latin text on the Vatican website reads: "… taking into account that the location of the religious himself or herself *may be unknown*."[3]

Other languages that translate this Latin phrase make it sound like "may" is supposed to be "must" in the English translation, which changes the meaning of this section. Did the Holy Father intend to make the twelve-month absence that triggers *ipso facto* dismissal to apply only when the member is not able to be located?

Thank you for any help that you can shed on the accurate translation of this phrase.

---

[1] See *Roman Replies and CLSA Advisory Opinions 2019*, page 25, for the text of this document.

[2] See http://w2.vatican.va/content/francesco/la/motu_proprio/documents/papa-francesco-motu-proprio-20190319_communis-vita.html (accessed on 28 September 2020).

[3] See http://www.vatican.va/content/francesco/en/motu_proprio/documents/papa-frances co-motu-proprio-20190319_communis-vita.html (emphasis added) (accessed on 28 September 2020).

RESPONSE

Pontificio Consiglio per i Testi Legislativi
Question about application of m.p. *Communis vita*
Vatican City

May 11, 2020

Dear _____,

Thank you for your email in which you present the difficulty to interpret *Communis vita* in the right way.

Regrettably, the English translation is not correct! The presupposition is that the religious cannot be located and his/her whereabouts are not known. If they'd be known, the procedure of can. 696 with admonition etc., could be easily followed. The reason why this new ground for *ipso facto* demission was introduced has been the difficulty to locate the religious who are illegitimately absent and invite them to come back or start the process of demission.

Hoping that these clarifications have been helpful to you I send my best regards,

/s/
Under-Secretary

This explanation was supported by the release of the "Circular Letter on the Motu Proprio of Pope Francis Communis vita," by the Congregation for Institutes of Consecrated Life and Societies of Apostolic Life on 8 September 2019. The English text of that circular letter follows.

Original Italian Text

Congregatio pro Institutis vitae consecrate
et Societatibus vitae apostolicae

Litterae circulares de Litteris Apostolicis Motu Proprio datis
«Communis vita»

Alle Moderatrici e ai Moderatori Generali;

Siamo consapevoli che la fisionomia della vita fraterna in comune «rivela molte trasformazioni rispetto al passato. Tali trasformazioni, come anche le speranze e le disillusioni che le hanno accompagnate e continuano ad accompagnarle, richiedono una riflessione alla luce del Concilio Vaticano II. Esse hanno condotto a effetti positivi, ma anche ad altri piu discutibili. Hanno messo in luce non pochi valori evangelici, dando nuova vitalita alla comunita religiosa, ma hanno anche suscitato interrogativi per aver oscurato alcuni elementi tipici della medesima vita fraterna vissuta in comunita. In alcuni luoghi sembra che la comunita religiosa abbia perso rilevanza agli oc-chi dei religiosi e religiose e forse non sia più un ideale da perseguire».

Così l'Istruzione *La vita fraterna in comunità*, pubblicata dalla Congregazione per gli Istituti di vita consacrata e le Società di vita apostolica il 2 febbraio 1994. Documento che, a distanza di tempo, rimane attuale, in particolare nella disamina degli effetti positivi e di quelli più discutibili nell'e-sperienza della vita comune.

Tra questi ultimi meritano particolare attenzione i casi di assenza illegittima dalla comunità e irreperibilità del religioso/a. Il m.p. *Communis vita* di Papa Francesco - promulgato il 19 marzo del corrente anno - che ha modificato il can. 694 del Codice di Diritto Canonico, va compreso nel contesto degli effetti discutibili di una presa di distanza da un aspetto cardine dell'identità religiosa. Al § 1 del can. 694 è stato inserito un terzo motivo di dimissione *ipso facto* dall'istituto religioso: l'assenza illegittima dalla casa religiosa protratta, ai sensi del can. 665 § 2, per dodici mesi ininterrotti, unitamente alla irreperibilità del religioso stesso.

Nel *motu proprio* il Santo Padre ha precisato, aggiungendo il § 3, la procedura da seguire nei casi in cui si applica la nuova fattispecie di dimissione, integrando quella descritta al § 2 del medesimo canone, rimasto invariato. Tale modifica offre l'opportunità di trovare una soluzione ai casi di assenza illegittima, con particolare riferimento ai sodali che a volte non possono edssere rintracciati o che si sono resi irreperibili.

1. La Congregazione per gli Istituti di vita consacrata e le Società di vita apostolica, nel quotidiano esercizio dei suoi compiti ha evidenziato, in particolare, alcune situazioni:

- religiosi/e che si sono allontanati dalla casa religiosa senza licenza del proprio superiore, ovvero, illegittimamente con l'intenzione di sottrarsi alla potesta dei superiori (cfr. can. 665 § 2);
- religiosi/e che, ottenuto il permesso di assenza legittima (cfr. can. 665 § 1) o la concessione di indulto di esclaustrazione (cfr. can. 686 § 1), allo scadere del termine, non hanno fatto ritorno in comunità;

– religiosi/e che, allontanatisi illegittimamente, si sono resi irreperibili, ovvero non hanno comunicato al Superiore il proprio il recapito, o la dimora, o almeno indicazioni certe della propria reperibilità.

2. Pertanto il can. 694 § 1, 3° si applica esclusivamente ai religiosi/e e ai sodali delle Società di vita apostolica assenti illegittimamente e irreperibili. Non si applica:

– ai religiosi/e assenti legittimamente ma irreperibili;
– ai religiosi/e assenti illegittimamente, ma reperibili.

Si considera irreperibile la persona di cui si conosca solo:

– il recapito telefonico;
– l'indirizzo di posta elettronica;
– il profilo sui social network;
– l'indirizzo fittizio.

3. Il Superiore Maggiore ha il dovere di cercare il religioso/a assente illegittimamente e irreperibile mediante la richiesta di informazioni:

– ai confratelli/ consorelle, ai precedenti Superiori Maggiori, ai Vescovi, al clero locale, ai familiari o parenti;
– alle istanze delle autorità civili nel rispetto della legislazione nazionale e della normativa sulla *privacy*.

Il Superiore competente non limita il suo impegno a saltuarie e affrettate indagini, ma esprime la sua sollecitudine verso il religioso/a perché ritorni e perseveri nella propria vocazione (cfr. can. 665 § 2).

4. Sovente i risultati delle ricerche danno esito negativo, anche se reiterate nel tempo. Altre volte si deve prendere atto che i sodali si rendono volutamente irreperibili. I Superiori competenti, di fronte a queste situazioni, hanno chiesto al Dicastero come comportarsi per «dare certezza giuridica alla situazione di fatto».

A tal fine, è utile precisare che il Superiore competente:

– è tenuto a produrre prova certa, mediante documentazione verificabile, delle ricerche espletate, dei tentativi di contatto o comunicazione;
– di fronte all'esito negativo delle ricerche, procede alla dichiarazione di irreperibilità del sodale.

5. Il Superiore competente valuta il caso con il suo Consiglio ed emette una dichiarazione di irreperibilità. Tale dichiarazione è resa necessaria per la certezza del computo del tempo:

–   del giorno a *quo*, a partire dal quale si prende atto dell'irreperibilita (cfr. can. 203 § 1), che non può rimanere incerto perché renderebbe indefi-nito il periodo di dodici mesi continui;
–   della decorrenza dei termini per fissare la scadenza dei dodici mesi continui.

6. Trascorsi dodici mesi continui, durante i quali non fosse, in alcun modo, cambiata la situazione di irreperibilità del sodale assente illegittimamente, il Superiore competente deve procedere alla *dichiarazione del fatto* perchè consti giuridicamente la dimissione a norma del can. 694. Tale dichiarazione deve essere confermata dalla Santa Sede se l'Istituto da cui il sodale viene dimesso è di diritto pontificio, mentre deve essere confermata dal Vescovo della sede principale se l'Istituto e di diritto diocesano.

7. Il nuovo dispositivo (can. 694 § 1, 3°) non si applica alle fattispecie antecedenti il 10 aprile 2019, in altri termini non può dirsi retroattivo, diversamente il Legislatore lo avrebbe dovuto dichiarare espressamente (cfr. can. 9).

Il m.p. *Communis vita* ha comportato la modifica del can. 729 che regola la vita degli istituti secolari, perche ai membri di tali istituti non si applica la dimissione dall'istituto per assenza illegittima.

Auspicando una corretta applicazione del terzo comma del § 1 del can. 694, il Dicastero invita i Superiori Maggiori ad avvalersi delle indicazioni attuative qui formulate, nella consapevolezza che i religiosi/e sono «chiamati ad offrire un modello concreto di comunità - come afferma Papa Francesco nella *Lettera Apostolica ai consacrati* (21 novembre 2014) -, che attraverso il riconoscimento della dignità di ogni persona e nella condivisione del dono di cui ognuno è portatore, permetta di vivere rapporti fraterni».

Citta del Vaticano, 8 settembre 2019, Natività della Beata Vergine Maria

JOÁO BRAZ *Card.* DE AVIZ
Prefetto

✠JOSÉ RODRÌGUEZ CARBALLO, O.F.M.
Arcivescovo Segretario

Congregation for Institutes of Consecrated Life
and Societies of Apostolic Life

Circular Letter on the apostolic letter motu proprio
Communis vita

To all general moderators,

We are aware that the expression of life in community "reveals many transformations of what was lived in the past. These transformations, as well as the hopes and disappointments which have accompanied them, and continue to do so, require reflection in light of the Second Vatican Council. The transformations have led to positive results, but also to results which are questionable. They have put into a clearer light not a few Gospel values, thus giving new vitality to religious community, but they have also given rise to questions by obscuring some elements characteristic of this same fraternal life lived in community. In some places, it seems that religious community has lost its relevance in the eyes of women and men religious and is, perhaps, no longer an ideal to be pursued." This resulted in the Instruction *"Fraternal life in community"* published by this *Congregation for Institutes of Consecrated Life and Society of Apostolic Life* on 2 February 1994. It is a document which, despite the passage of time, remains relevant in the examination of both the positive and more questionable aspects in the experience of life lived in common.

Among these are cases of illegitimate absence from community joined with the inability of contacting the religious. The m.p. *Communis vita* of Pope Francis -promulgated on March 19 of this year - which modified can. 694 of the Code of Canon Law addresses the questionable aspect of distancing oneself from community, an essential element of religious identity. A third reason for *ipso facto* dismissal from a religious Institute has been added to §1 of can. 694: a protracted illegitimate absence from a religious house, for twelve uninterrupted months in accord with can. 665 §2, together with the inability of contacting the religious.

In the *motu proprio*, which added §3, the Holy Father clarified the procedure to be followed in the new reason for dismissal, integrating what. is already described in §2 of the same canon, which remained unchanged. The aforementioned change offers the opportunity to find a solution to the cases of illegitimate absence with particular reference to members who "sometimes cannot be located" and who, therefore, are not able to be contacted.

1. The Congregation for Institutes of Consecrated Life and Societies of Apostolic Life, in the exercise of its daily tasks has highlighted, some situations, in particular:

- Members of religious institutes, male and female, who have left the religious house without permission from their superior, or, illegitimatelywith the intention of avoiding the power of the superiors (cf. can. 665 §2);
- religious who, having obtained the permission of legitimate absence (cf. can. 665 §1) or the granting of an indult of exclaustration (cf. can. 686 §1), did not return to the community at the expiration of the term;
- religious who, having left illegitimately, have become unable to be contacted, or have not communicated to the Superior his/her address or place of residence, or at least some indications of how he/she may be contacted.

2. Therefore, can. 694 §1, 3° applies exclusively to religious and members of a Society of apostolic life, who are illegitimately absent and not able to be contacted. It does not apply to:

- religious who are legitimately absent but cannot be found;
- religious who are illegitimately absent but are able to be contacted;

A person is to be considered unable to be contacted if one knows only:

- a telephone number
- an e-mail address
- a profile on social networks
- a fictitious address

3. The Major Superior has the duty to look for the religious who is absent illegitimately and cannot be found by requesting information:

- from confreres, sisters, the previous Major Superiors, Bishops, local clergy, family members and relatives;
- In cases of civil authorities in compliance with national legislation and privacy legislation.

The commitment of the competent Superior is not limited to occasional and hasty inquiries, but rather is to be a research that truly expresses his/her concern for the religious so that he/she may return to community and persevere in his/her own vocation (cf. can. 665 §2).

4. Often the results of the research give negative results, even if repeated over time. At other times, however, it must be acknowledged that members are

intentionally not able to be contacted. The competent Superiors, faced with these situations, have asked the Dicastery how to behave on order to "give legal certainty to the de facto situation".

To respond to this it is useful to clarify that the competent Superior:

- has to produce certain proof through verifiable documentation of the research carried out and of the attempts at contacting or communicating with the member.
- in the face of a negative outcome of the aforementioned research, the competent Superior proceeds with the declaration of the inability to contact the member.

5. The competent Superior evaluates the case with his/her Council and issues a declaration of inability to be contacted. This declaration is necessary for the certainty of the accounting of time:

- the day *a quo* from which the religious cannot be found cannot remain uncertain, because it would make the twelve continuous month period undefined (cf. can. 203 §1);
- the expiration of the terms to fix the deadline of the twelve continuous months.

6. Once the twelve months have elapsed, during which the situation of unavailability of the illegitimate absentee was not changed in any way, the competent Superior must proceed to the *declaration of the fact* to legally establish the *ipso facto* dismissal according to the norm of can. 694.

In order for the dismissal to be legally valid, this declaration must be confirmed by the Holy See if the Institute from which the member is dismissed is of Pontifical Right, while it must be confirmed by the Bishop of the principal seat if the Institute is of Diocesan Right.

The new provision (can. 694 §1, 3°) does not apply to cases prior to 10 April 2019, in other words it cannot be said to be retroactive, otherwise the Legislator should have expressly declared it (cf. can. 9). The m.p. *Communis vita* called for the modification of can. 729 which regulates the life of secular institutes, because dismissal from the Institute for illegitimate absence does not apply to members of such Institutes.

Hoping for the correct application of the third paragraph of can. 694, the Dicastery invites Major Superiors to make use of the implementation instructions formulated here, aware that religious are "called to offer a concrete model of community which, by acknowledging the dignity of each person and sharing our respective gifts, makes it possible to live as brothers and sisters", as Pope Francis states in the *Apostolic Letter to consecrated persons* (21 November 2014).

Vatican City, 8 September 2019
Nativity of the Blessed Virgin Mary

JOÁO BRAZ Card. de Aviz
Prefect

✠JOSÉ RODRÌGUEZ CARBALLO, O.F.M.
Archbishop Secretary

CANON 850; *RITUALE ROMANO*

THE VALIDITY OF BAPTISMS ADMINISTERED WITH WORDS OTHER THAN THOSE PRESCRIBED IN THE APPROVED LITURGICAL BOOKS IN CASES THAT DO NOT INVOLVE URGENT NECESSITY

Recently the Congregation for the Doctrine of the Faith has dealt with some cases of administration of the sacrament of Baptism in which the sacramental formula established by the Church in the liturgical books has been arbitrarily modified. For this reason, the Dicastery has prepared "Answers to proposed questions," with its "Doctrinal Note" which explains its content, to recall the doctrine about the validity of the sacraments connected to the form established by the Church with the use of approved sacramental formulas, in order to remove the issue from deviant interpretations and practices and offer a clear orientation.

RESPONSE

"Responsum" della Congregazione per la Dottrina della Fede ad un dubbio sulla validità del Battesimo conferito con la formula "Noi ti battezziamo nel nome del Padre e del Figlio e dello Spirito Santo," 06.08.2020

Recentemente la Congregazione per la Dottrina della Fede ha trattato alcuni casi di amministrazione del sacramento del Battesimo nei quali è stata arbitrariamente modificata la formula sacramentale stabilita dalla Chiesa nei libri liturgici.

Per tale motivo, il Dicastero ha preparato "Risposte a quesiti proposti", con relativa "Nota dottrinale" che ne spiega il contenuto, per richiamare la dottrina circa la validità dei sacramenti connessa alla forma stabilita dalla Chiesa con l'uso delle formule sacramentali approvate, al fine di sottrarre la questione ad interpretazioni e prassi devianti e offrire un chiaro orientamento.

RISPOSTE A QUESITI PROPOSTI

sulla validità del Battesimo conferito con la formula
«Noi ti battezziamo nel nome del Padre e del Figlio e dello Spirito Santo»

QUESITI

Primo: È valido il Battesimo conferito con la formula: «Noi ti battezziamo nel nome del Padre e del Figlio e dello Spirito Santo»?

Secondo: Coloro per i quali è stato celebrato il Battesimo con la suddetta formula devono essere battezzati in forma assoluta?

RISPOSTE

Al primo: Negativamente.

Al secondo: Affermativamente.

Il Sommo Pontefice Francesco, nel corso dell'Udienza concessa al sottoscritto Cardinale Prefetto, in data 8 giugno 2020, ha approvato queste Risposte e ne ha ordinato la pubblicazione.

Dalla sede della Congregazione per la Dottrina della Fede, il 24 giugno 2020, nella Solennità della Natività di san Giovanni Battista.

Luis F. Card. Ladaria, S.I.
Prefetto

✠ Giacomo Morandi
Arcivescovo tit. di Cerveteri
Segretario

* * *

NOTA DOTTRINALE
circa la modifica della formula sacramentale del Battesimo

Recentemente vi sono state celebrazioni del Sacramento del Battesimo amministrato con le parole: «A nome del papà e della mamma, del padrino e della madrina, dei nonni, dei familiari, degli amici, a nome della comunità noi ti battezziamo nel nome del Padre e del Figlio e dello Spirito Santo». A quanto sembra, la deliberata modifica della formula sacramentale è stata introdotta per sottolineare il valore comunitario del Battesimo, per esprimere la partecipazione della famiglia e dei presenti e per evitare l'idea della concentrazione di un potere sacrale nel sacerdote a discapito dei genitori e della comunità, che la formula presente nel Rituale Romano veicolerebbe.[1] Riaffiora qui, con discutibili

---

[1] In realtà, un'attenta analisi del Rito del Battesimo dei Bambini mostra che nella celebrazione i genitori, i padrini e l'intera comunità sono chiamati a svolgere un ruolo attivo, un vero e proprio ufficio liturgico (cfr. Rituale Romanum ex Decreto Sacrosancti Oecumenici Concilii Vaticani II instauratum auctoritate Pauli PP. VI promulgatum, Ordo Baptismi Parvulorum, Praenotanda, nn. 4-7), che secondo il dettato conciliare comporta però che «ciascuno, ministro o fedele, svolgendo il proprio ufficio, compia soltanto e tutto

motivazioni di ordine pastorale,[2] un'antica tentazione di sostituire la formula consegnata dalla Tradizione con altri testi giudicati più idonei. A tale riguardo già San Tommaso d'Aquino si era posto la questione «utrum plures possint simul baptizare unum et eundem» alla quale aveva risposto negativamente in quanto prassi contraria alla natura del ministro.[3]

Il Concilio Vaticano II asserisce che: «Quando uno battezza è Cristo stesso che battezza».[4] L'affermazione della Costituzione sulla sacra liturgia Sacrosanctum Concilium, ispirata a un testo di sant'Agostino,[5] vuole ricondurre la celebrazione sacramentale alla presenza di Cristo, non solo nel senso che egli vi trasfonde la sua virtus per donarle efficacia, ma soprattutto per indicare che il Signore è il protagonista dell'evento che si celebra.

La Chiesa infatti, quando celebra un Sacramento, agisce come Corpo che opera inseparabilmente dal suo Capo, in quanto è Cristo-Capo che agisce nel Corpo ecclesiale da lui generato nel mistero della Pasqua.[6] La dottrina dell'istituzione divina dei Sacramenti, solennemente affermata dal Concilio di Trento,[7] vede così il suo naturale sviluppo e la sua autentica interpretazione nella citata affermazione di Sacrosanctum Concilium. I due Concili si trovano quindi in complementare sintonia nel dichiarare l'assoluta indisponibilità del settenario sacramentale all'azione della Chiesa. I Sacramenti, infatti, in quanto istituiti da Gesù Cristo, sono affidati alla Chiesa perché siano da essa custoditi. Appare qui evidente che la Chiesa, sebbene sia costituita dallo Spirito Santo interprete della Parola di Dio e possa in una certa misura determinare i riti che esprimono la grazia sacramentale offerta da Cristo, non dispone dei fondamenti stessi del suo esistere: la Parola di Dio e i gesti salvifici di Cristo.

---

quello che, secondo la natura del rito e le norme liturgiche, è di sua competenza»: Concilio Ecumenico Vaticano II, Cost. Sacrosanctum Concilium, n. 28.

[2] Spesso il ricorso alla motivazione pastorale maschera, anche inconsapevolmente, una deriva soggettivistica e una volontà manipolatrice. Già nel secolo scorso Romano Guardini ricordava che se nella preghiera personale il credente può seguire l'impulso del cuore, nell'azione liturgica «deve aprirsi a un altro impulso, di più possente e profonda origine, venuto dal cuore della Chiesa che batte attraverso i secoli. Qui non conta ciò che personalmente gli piace o in quel momento gli sembra desiderabile...» (R. Guardini, Vorschule des Betens, Einsiedeln/Zürich, 1948², p. 258; trad. it.: Introduzione alla preghiera, Brescia 2009, p. 196).

[3] Summa Theologiae, III, q. 67, a. 6 c.

[4] Concilio Ecumenico Vaticano II, Cost. Sacrosanctum Concilium, n. 7.

[5] S. Augustinus, In Evangelium Ioannis tractatus, VI, 7.

[6] Cfr. Concilio Ecumenico Vaticano II, Cost. Sacrosanctum Concilium, n. 5.

[7] Cfr. DH, n. 1601.

Risulta pertanto comprensibile come nel corso dei secoli la Chiesa abbia custodito con cura la forma celebrativa dei Sacramenti, soprattutto in quegli elementi che la Scrittura attesta e che permettono di riconoscere con assoluta evidenza il gesto di Cristo nell'azione rituale della Chiesa. Il Concilio Vaticano II ha inoltre stabilito che nessuno «anche se sacerdote, osi, di sua iniziativa, aggiungere, togliere o mutare alcunché in materia liturgica».[8] Modificare di propria iniziativa la forma celebrativa di un Sacramento non costituisce un semplice abuso liturgico, come trasgressione di una norma positiva, ma un vulnus inferto a un tempo alla comunione ecclesiale e alla riconoscibilità dell'azione di Cristo, che nei casi più gravi rende invalido il Sacramento stesso, perché la natura dell'azione ministeriale esige di trasmettere con fedeltà quello che si è ricevuto (cfr. 1 Cor 15, 3).

Nella celebrazione dei Sacramenti, infatti, il soggetto è la Chiesa-Corpo di Cristo insieme al suo Capo, che si manifesta nella concreta assemblea radunata.[9] Tale assemblea però agisce ministerialmente – non collegialmente – perché nessun gruppo può fare di se stesso Chiesa, ma diviene Chiesa in virtù di una chiamata che non può sorgere dall'interno dell'assemblea stessa. Il ministro è quindi segno-presenza di Colui che raduna e, al tempo stesso, luogo di comunione di ogni assemblea liturgica con la Chiesa tutta. In altre parole, il ministro è un segno esteriore della sottrazione del Sacramento al nostro disporne e del suo carattere relativo alla Chiesa universale.

In questa luce va compreso il dettato tridentino sulla necessità del ministro di avere l'intenzione almeno di fare quello che fa la Chiesa.[10] L'intenzione non può però rimanere solo a livello interiore, con il rischio di derive soggettivistiche, ma si esprime nell'atto esteriore che viene posto, con l'utilizzo della materia e della forma del Sacramento. Tale atto non può che manifestare la comunione tra ciò che il ministro compie nella celebrazione di ogni singolo Sacramento con ciò che la Chiesa svolge in comunione con l'azione di Cristo stesso: è perciò fondamentale che l'azione sacramentale sia compiuta non in nome proprio, ma nella persona di Cristo, che agisce nella sua Chiesa, e in nome della Chiesa.

Pertanto, nel caso specifico del Sacramento del Battesimo, il ministro non solo non ha l'autorità di disporre a suo piacimento della formula sacramentale, per i motivi di natura cristologica ed ecclesiologica sopra esposti, ma non può nemmeno dichiarare di agire a nome dei genitori, dei padrini, dei familiari o degli amici, e nemmeno a nome della stessa assemblea radunata per la celebrazione,

---

[8] Concilio Ecumenico Vaticano II, Cost. Sacrosanctum Concilium, n. 22 § 3.
[9] Cfr. Catechismus Catholicae Ecclesiae, n. 1140: «Tota communitas, corpus Christi suo Capiti unitum, celebrat» e n. 1141: «Celebrans congregatio communitas est baptizatorum».
[10] Cfr. DH, n. 1611.

perché il ministro agisce in quanto segno-presenza dell'azione stessa di Cristo che si compie nel gesto rituale della Chiesa. Quando il ministro dice «Io ti battezzo…» non parla come un funzionario che svolge un ruolo affidatogli, ma opera ministerialmente come segno-presenza di Cristo, che agisce nel suo Corpo, donando la sua grazia e rendendo quella concreta assemblea liturgica manifestazione «della genuina natura della vera Chiesa»[11], in quanto «le azioni liturgiche non sono azioni private, ma celebrazioni della Chiesa, che è sacramento di unità, cioè popolo santo radunato e ordinato sotto la guida dei vescovi».[12]

Alterare la formula sacramentale significa, inoltre, non comprendere la natura stessa del ministero ecclesiale, che è sempre servizio a Dio e al suo popolo e non esercizio di un potere che giunge alla manipolazione di ciò che è stato affidato alla Chiesa con un atto che appartiene alla Tradizione. In ogni ministro del Battesimo deve essere quindi radicata non solo la consapevolezza di dover agire nella comunione ecclesiale, ma anche la stessa convinzione che sant'Agostino attribuisce al Precursore, il quale «apprese che ci sarebbe stata in Cristo una proprietà tale per cui, malgrado la moltitudine dei ministri, santi o peccatori, che avrebbero battezzato, la santità del Battesimo non era da attribuirsi se non a colui sopra il quale discese la colomba, e del quale fu detto: "È lui quello che battezza nello Spirito Santo" (Gv 1, 33)». Quindi, commenta Agostino: «Battezzi pure Pietro, è Cristo che battezza; battezzi Paolo, è Cristo che battezza; e battezzi anche Giuda, è Cristo che battezza».[13]

Unofficial Translation

RESPONSES TO QUESTIONS PROPOSED
on the validity of Baptism conferred with the formula
"We baptize you in the name of the Father and of the Son
and of the Holy Spirit"

QUESTIONS

First question: Whether the Baptism conferred with the formula "We baptize you in the name of the Father and of the Son and of the Holy Spirit" is valid?

---

[11] Concilio Ecumenico Vaticano II, Cost. Sacrosanctum Concilium, n. 2.
[12] Ibidem, n. 26.
[13] S. Augustinus, In Evangelium Ioannis tractatus, VI, 7.

Second question: Whether those persons for whom baptism was celebrated with this formula must be baptized *in forma absoluta*?

RESPONSES

To the first question: Negative.

To the second question: Affirmative.

The Supreme Pontiff Francis, at the Audience granted to the undersigned Cardinal Prefect of the Congregation for the Doctrine of the Faith, on June 8, 2020, approved these Responses and ordered their publication.

Rome, from the Offices of the Congregation for the Doctrine of the Faith, June 24, 2020, on the Solemnity of the Nativity of Saint John the Baptist.

Luis F. Card. Ladaria, S.I.
Prefect

✠ Giacomo Morandi
Titular Archbishop of Cerveteri
Secretary

* * *

DOCTRINAL NOTE
on the modification of the sacramental formula of Baptism

Recently there have been celebrations of the Sacrament of Baptism administered with the words: "In the name of the father and of the mother, of the godfather and of the godmother, of the grandparents, of the family members, of the friends, in the name of the community we baptize you in the name of the Father and of the Son and of the Holy Spirit." Apparently, the deliberate modification of the sacramental formula was introduced to emphasize the communitarian significance of Baptism, in order to express the participation of the family and of those present, and to avoid the idea of the concentration of a sacred power in the priest to the detriment of the parents and the community that the formula in the *Rituale*

Romano might seem to imply.[1] With debatable pastoral motives,[2] here resurfaces the ancient temptation to substitute for the formula handed down by Tradition other texts judged more suitable. In this regard, St. Thomas Aquinas had already asked himself the question "*utrum plures possint simul baptizare unum et eundem*" to which he had replied negatively, insofar as this practice is contrary to the nature of the minister.[3]

The Second Vatican Council states that: "when a man baptizes it is really Christ Himself who baptizes."[4] The affirmation of the Constitution on the Sacred Liturgy *Sacrosanctum Concilium*, inspired by a text of Saint Augustine,[5] wants to return the sacramental celebration to the presence of Christ, not only in the sense that he infuses his *virtus* to give it efficacy, but above all to indicate that the Lord has the principal role in the event being celebrated.

When celebrating a Sacrament, the Church in fact functions as the Body that acts inseparably from its Head, since it is Christ the Head who acts in the ecclesial Body generated by him in the Paschal mystery.[6] The doctrine of the divine institution of the Sacraments, solemnly affirmed by the Council of Trent,[7] thus sees its natural development and authentic interpretation in the above-mentioned affirmation of *Sacrosanctum Concilium*. The two Councils are therefore in harmony in declaring that they do not have the authority to subject the seven sacraments to the action of the Church. The Sacraments, in fact, inasmuch as they were instituted by Jesus Christ, are entrusted to the Church to be preserved by her.

---

[1]   In reality, a careful analysis of the *Rite of Baptism of Children* shows that in the celebration the parents, godparents and the entire community are called to play an active role, a true liturgical office (cf. Rituale Romanum *ex Decreto Sacrosancti Oecumenici Concilii Vaticani II instauratum auctoritate Pauli PP. VI promulgatum, Ordo Baptismi Parvulorum, Praenotanda*, nn. 4-7), which according to the conciliar provisions, however, requires that "each person, minister or layman, who has an office to perform, should do all of, but only, those parts which pertain to his office by the nature of the rite and the principles of liturgy" (Second Vatican Ecumenical Council, Constitution on the Sacred Liturgy *Sacrosanctum Concilium*, 28).

[2]   Often the recourse to pastoral motivation masks, even unconsciously, a subjective deviation and a manipulative will. Already in the last century Romano Guardini recalled that if in personal prayer the believer can follow the impulse of the heart, in liturgical action "he must open himself to a different kind of impulse which comes from a more powerful source: namely, the heart of the Church which beats through the ages. Here it does not matter what personal tastes are, what wants he may have, or what particular cares occupy his mind..." (R. Guardini, *Vorschule des Betens*, Einsiedeln/Zürich, 1948², p. 258; Eng. trans.: *The Art of Praying*, Manchester, NH, 1985, 176).

[3]   *Summa Theologiae*, III, q. 67, a. 6 c.

[4]   Second Vatican Ecumenical Council, Constitution *Sacrosanctum Concilium*, 7.

[5]   S. Augustinus, *In Evangelium Ioannis tractatus*, VI, 7.

[6]   Cf. Second Vatican Ecumenical Council, Constitution Sacrosanctum Concilium, 5.

[7]   Cf. DH 1601.

It is evident here that although the Church is constituted by the Holy Spirit, who is the interpreter of the Word of God, and can, to a certain extent, determine the rites which express the sacramental grace offered by Christ, does not establish the very foundations of her existence: the Word of God and the saving acts of Christ.

It is therefore understandable that in the course of the centuries the Church has safeguarded the form of the celebration of the Sacraments, above all in those elements to which Scripture attests and that make it possible to recognize with absolute clarity the gesture of Christ in the ritual action of the Church. The Second Vatican Council has likewise established that no one "even if he be a priest, may add, remove, or change anything in the liturgy on his own authority."[8] Modifying on one's own initiative the form of the celebration of a Sacrament does not constitute simply a liturgical abuse, like the transgression of a positive norm, but a *vulnus* inflicted upon the ecclesial communion and the identifiability of Christ's action, and in the most grave cases rendering invalid the Sacrament itself, because the nature of the ministerial action requires the transmission with fidelity of that which has been received (cf. 1 Cor 15:3).

In the celebration of the Sacraments, in fact, the subject is the Church, the Body of Christ together with its Head, that manifests itself in the concrete gathered assembly.[9] Such an assembly therefore acts *ministerially* – not collegially – because no group can make itself Church, but becomes Church in virtue of a call that cannot arise from within the assembly itself. The minister is therefore the sign-presence of Him who gathers and is at the same time the locus of the communion of every liturgical assembly with the whole Church. In other words, the minister is the visible sign that the Sacrament is not subject to an arbitrary action of individuals or of the community, and that it pertains to the Universal Church.

In this light must be understood the tridentine injunction concerning the necessity of the minister to at least have the intention to do that which the Church does.[10] The intention therefore cannot remain only at the interior level, with the risk of subjective distractions, but must be expressed in the exterior action constituted by the use of the matter and form of the Sacrament. Such an action cannot but manifest the communion between that which the minister accomplishes in the celebration of each individual sacrament with that which the Church enacts in communion with the action of Christ himself: It is therefore fundamental that the sacramental action may not be achieved in its own name, but in the person of Christ who acts in his Church, and in the name of the Church.

---

[8] Second Vatican Ecumenical Council, Constitution *Sacrosanctum Concilium*, 22 § 3.

[9] Cf. *Catechismus Catholicae Ecclesiae*, n. 1140: "Tota communitas, corpus Christi suo Capiti unitum, celebrat" and 1141: "Celebrans congregatio communitas est baptizatorum."

[10] Cf. DH 1611.

Therefore, in the specific case of the Sacrament of Baptism, not only does the minister not have the authority to modify the sacramental formula to his own liking, for the reasons of a christological and ecclesiological nature already articulated, but neither can he even declare that he is acting on behalf of the parents, godparents, relatives or friends, nor in the name of the assembly gathered for the celebration, because he acts insofar as he is the sign-presence of the same Christ that is enacted in the ritual gesture of the Church. When the minister says "I baptize you..." he does not speak as a functionary who carries out a role entrusted to him, but he enacts *ministerially* the sign-presence of Christ, who acts in his Body to give his grace and to make the concrete liturgical assembly a manifestation of "the real nature of the true Church,"[11] insofar as "liturgical services are not private functions, but are celebrations of the Church, which is the 'sacrament of unity,' namely the holy people united and ordered under their bishops."[12]

Moreover, to modify the sacramental formula implies a lack of an understanding of the very nature of the ecclesial ministry that is always at the service of God and his people and not the exercise of a power that goes so far as to manipulate what has been entrusted to the Church in an act that pertains to the Tradition. Therefore, in every minister of Baptism, there must not only be a deeply rooted knowledge of the obligation to act in ecclesial communion, but also the same conviction that Saint Augustine attributes to the Precursor, which "was to be a certain peculiarity in Christ, such that, although many ministers, be they righteous or unrighteous, should baptize, the virtue of Baptism would be attributed to Him alone on whom the dove descended, and of whom it was said: 'It is he who baptizes with the Holy Spirit' (*Jn* 1:33)." Therefore, Augustine comments: "Peter may baptize, but this is He that baptizes; Paul may baptize, yet this is He that baptizes; Judas may baptize, still this is He that baptizes."[13]

NOTE: This unofficial English translation is published on the Vatican website at http://w2.vatican.va/content/francesco/en/motu_proprio/documents/papa-france sco-motu-proprio-20190319_communis-vita.html (accessed on 28 September 2020).

---

[11] Second Vatican Ecumenical Council, Constitution *Sacrosanctum Concilium*, 2.
[12] Ibid., 26.
[13] S. Augustinus, *In Evangelium Ioannis tractatus*, VI, 7.

Canons 976 and 986 §2

Right of Accused Cleric to Petition for Dispensation from Clerical Obligations

*The "*Vademecum *on Certain Points of Procedure in Treating Cases of Sexual Abuse of Minors Committed by Clerics" issued by the Congregation for the Doctrine of the Faith on 16 July 2020, points out in paragraph 157 that an accused cleric has the right to present a petition to the Holy Father to be dispensed from all obligations connected with the clerical state, including celibacy. It further states that the Ordinary is obligated to inform the accused cleric of this right. This is a sample of the rescript issued in response to such a petition.* [1]

RESPONSE

Congregation for the Doctrine of the Faith

Prot. N. xxx/xxxx

Dioecesim
(Diocese, USA)

Mr. N.N., presbyter of this diocese

———————————

The Supreme Pontiff, Pope Francis
on 29 July 2020

after considering a report on this case from the Congregation for the Doctrine of the Faith, agrees to the petition of the above-mentioned presbyter *for the good of the Church* and grants a dispensation from the obligations of the priesthood together with a dispensation from sacred celibacy according to the following procedures:

1. The petitioner is to be notified of the rescript of dispensation by the Ordinary as soon as possible:

    a)   It takes effect from the moment of notification;

    b)   The rescript inseparably includes a dispensation from sacred celibacy and the loss of the clerical state at the same time. It is never permitted for the petitioner to separate the two elements, or to accept one and refuse the other;

---

[1] Translation by Rev. W. Becket Soule, O.P.

c)   This rescript carries with it, to the extent necessary, absolution from censures.

2. The notification of this rescript can be made by the Ordinary himself or his delegate, or by an ecclesiastical notary, or by registered mail. The Ordinary must retain one copy, signed by the petitioner, in testimony of his receipt of the rescript of dispensation and of his acceptance of its provisions.

3. A notation of the granting of this dispensation is to be made in the baptismal register of the petitioner's parish.

4. With respect to the celebration of canonical marriage, if the case warrants, the norms established by the *Code of Canon Law* are to be applied. The Ordinary is to take care that the matter is handled carefully without any external pomp.

5. The ecclesiastical authority responsible for informing the petitioner of the rescript is strongly to encourage the petitioner to participate in the life of the People of God in a matter fitting his new condition of living, to be outstanding in his pursuits, and to show himself to be an upright son of the Church. He is to be informed of the following at the same time:

a)   A dispensed priest automatically loses rights proper to the clerical state, dignities, and ecclesiastical offices; he is no longer bound by other obligations connected to the clerical state;

b)   He remains excluded from the exercise of the sacred ministry, except for matters mentioned in cann. 976 and 986 §2 of the *Code of Canon Law*; furthermore, he cannot preach a homily, nor can he exercise a directive office in the pastoral sphere, nor be engaged in the function of parochial administration;

c)   He can fulfill no function in a seminary or in an equivalent institution. He cannot be engaged in any directive function in institutions of higher studies which are in any way dependent on ecclesiastical authority;

d)   He cannot teach any theological discipline in other institutions of higher studies which are not dependent on ecclesiastical authority;

e)   He is not, however, to be engaged in a directive function or teaching office in institutions of studies of a lower level which are dependent on ecclesiastical authority. A dispensed presbyter is bound by the same regulation in teaching religion in Institutes of the same type which are not dependent on ecclesiastical authority.

6. The Ordinary is to warn the petitioner, as he has been found unfit for ministry, not to act as a layman in the name of the Church. The petitioner is furthermore gravely bound in conscience to the obligation to make appropriate restitution of damages, where these exist.

7. The Ordinary is to take care, to the extent possible, that the condition of the dispensed presbyter not give scandal to the faithful. Nevertheless, if there is a

danger of abusing minors, the Ordinary is to divulge the fact of the dispensation and its canonical cause.

8. At an opportune time, the competent Ordinary is to send the Congregation a brief report of the notification which has taken place, and if there is still any wonderment among the faithful, he is to provide a prudent explanation.

All things to the contrary notwithstanding.

From the Office of the Congregation, 29 June 2020.

Luigi Francisco, Cardinal LADARIA, S.J.
       Prefect

✠Joseph Augustine DINOIA, O.P.
Titular Archbishop of Oregon City
       Adjunct Secretary

Date of notification _____

Signature of presbyter indicating acceptance _____

Signature of the Ordinary _____

Canons 1308-1310

Pious Foundations

A Mass foundation, about which only the title, the year of origin, and the subsequent bookkeeping was able to be located, no longer had sufficient funds to provide even a Mass a year at our customary Mass stipend amount. The Diocese requested from the Congregation for Clergy that the obligation be reduced. The Holy See's response is below.

Congregation pro Clericis

From the Vatican [DATE]

Prot. N.

Your Excellency,

This Congregation has received your letter and attachments, dated 11 May 2020, concerning the possible cessation of the Keenan Mass Foundation.

After careful study the Dicastery would offer the following indications. While the information surrounding the donor, is not all encompassing in relation to the present questions Your Excellency has presented, it is clear that the intention of the Foundation is a perpetual obligation to offer Masses for the intention of the donor.

To avoid the cessation of the Foundation the Diocese might approach some institution that does offer perpetual Masses and with the remaining donation have Masses offered in perpetuity for the intention of the donor. The fact of transfer would be kept on file at the Diocese.

I assure you of my prayerful solidarity, asking God to grant you every blessing, as I remain,

Yours sincerely in Christ,

✠ Beniamino Cardinal Stella Prefect

Canon 880 §1

Use of instruments for administering Confirmation during a pandemic

The Chairman of the United States Conference of Catholic Bishops Committee on Divine Worship submitted a dubium *in May of 2020 to the Congregation for Divine Worship and the Discipline of the Sacraments on the question of whether an instrument could be used in the anointing that is an essential part of the Sacrament of Confirmation.*

RESPONSE

By a letter dated June 2, the Congregation for Divine Worship and Discipline of the Sacraments replied as follows:

"The use by the minister of an instrument (gloves, cotton swab...), does not affect the validity of the Sacrament."[1]

---

[1] For the full letter see https://www.cathdal.org/USCCB-Confirmation-Letter-20200602.pdf.

CANONS 1478, 1481, 1505, 1508, AND 1545, AND *DIGNITAS CONNUBII* 97, 101, AND 127

REGARDING CITATION OF A VIOLENT RESPONDENT

INQUIRY

In keeping with Pastor Bonus article 124, 1°, the Metropolitan Tribunal of the Archdiocese of [ ] would be grateful for the assistance of the Supreme Tribunal of the Apostolic Signatura regarding [a] marriage nullity cause, which was admitted to the ordinary process in 2017 but thereafter renounced.

At the time the petitioner [ ] submitted her libellus, she declined to provide the address of the respondent and explained her deep concerns for her safety. She recounted how, approximately forty years ago, the respondent was incarcerated for kidnapping her and threatening murder. Although she did not corroborate this specific incident with documentation, she produced some third-party internet search results indicating possible criminal court cases for lesser offenses in the years since. The alleged offenses were not against her, and she had not produced proof of harm inflicted on her other than her account regarding the kidnapping forty years prior.

Ultimately, we concluded that the petitioner had not demonstrated the moral impossibility of citation or that the respondent currently was of diminished mental capacity necessitating citation through a curator, per canon 1478 §4. Having been advised of the need to cite the respondent, she renounced the cause.

Since then, she has requested that we revisit this decision, and we seek your direction regarding how best to proceed. Enclosed you will find an authentic copy of the Acts for your review.

RESPONSE

SUPREMUM SIGNATURAE APOSTOLICAE TRIBUNAL

23 January 2020

Dear Monsignor,

This Supreme Tribunal has received your letter dated 13 December 2019 wherein you ask guidance concerning the requested omission of the judicial citation in the above-captioned case.

This Apostolic Signatura is transmitting herewith the opinion of an expert who, having examined the acts submitted, has summarized the fundamental points of jurisprudence of this Supreme Tribunal on the matter.

I express my respect and esteem, and I remain

devotedly Yours in our Lord,

✠Giuseppe SCIACCA
Titular Bishop of Fondi
Secretary

***

EXPERT REPORT

On 13 December 2019, the Judicial Vicar of the Metropolitan Tribunal of [diocese] presented the above-captioned case, in which, after having been refused once already in 2017, the Petitioner again has requested that due to the danger of physical harm the case be instructed without the citation of the Respondent.

First and foremost the Reverend Judicial Vicar is to be commended for his discretion in the handling of this case, both in the fielding of the Petitioner's request and in the accepting of the *libellus*. Indeed, as the Reverend Adjunct Judicial Vicar stated in his letter of 14 July 2017, the omission of the Respondent's domicile is not a reason to reject the *libellus* (cf. can. 1505 §2 and art. 121 §1 of the Instruction *Dignitas connubii*), nor can the citation of the Respondent be omitted without gravely infringing on the party's right to defense.

With due consideration for the amount of time which has transpired since the events in question, it would seem strange if a copy of a restraining order, which was still in effect, could not easily be acquired from the competent civil authority. Indeed, after a prudential consultation with a civil lawyer, the judge may consider requesting that the Petitioner provide such documentation or otherwise an explanation as to why the documentation cannot be obtained (cf. can. 1545, and also art. 191 *DC* with due regard as well for art. 192 *DC*).

Otherwise, from the experience of the Apostolic Signatura, there are several ways-a few of which the Adjunct Judicial Vicar seems already aware-of carrying out the judicial citation of the Respondent that could eliminate or reduce any danger coming from the part of a violent Respondent. Such would include:

1. the constitution of a curator (guardian) for the Respondent when the judge, on the basis of elements in his possession, deems that the conditions contemplated by Canon Law occur (cf. can. 1478 and art. 97 *DC*);

2. the constitution of a procurator for the Respondent when the judge deems this necessary, always done according to canon law (cf. can. 1481 and art. 101 §2 *DC*;

3. refraining from communicating the address of the Petitioner to the Respondent;

4. refraining from sending a copy of the introductory petition (*libellus*) for the case (cf. can. 1508 §2 and art. 127 §3 *DC*);

5. requesting from the Apostolic Signatura a prorogation of competence, such that the process of the nullity of marriage may be celebrated in a locality that is distant from the residence of the Respondent or even of both parties (cf. art. 10 §4 DC).

Some examples of the jurisprudence of the Apostolic Signatura in this matter are collected in an article published in [G. Paoli Montini, "La Prassi Delle Dispense Da Leggi Processuali Del Supremo Tribunale Della Segnatura Apostolica (Art. 124, N. 2, 2a Parte, Cost. Ap. Pastor Bonus)"] *Periodica de re canonica* 94 (2005) [43-117] . . . .

CANON 1548 AND *VOS ESTIS LUX MUNDI*

REPORTING ACCUSATIONS AND PRIVACY ISSUES

The Pontifical Council for Legal Texts has provided an individual reply in answer to a late 2019 letter asking guidance for understanding and implementing Vos Estis Lux Mundi *articles 3, 4, and 19 and canon 1548, concerning issues of confidentiality. The inquiry predated the instruction concerning pontifical secret.* [1]

PONTIFICIUM CONSILIUM DE LEGUM TEXTIBUS

Prot. N.

Vatican City State, 06 February 2020

Dear Msgr.,

I write in reference to your letter of 30 November 2019 that arrived in our office on the 10th of January in which you requested this Pontifical Council to provide an opinion on properly understanding and implementing a particular article of the recent m.p. *Vos estis Lux Mundi*.

Your question concerns paragraph 1 of art. 4 of the m.p. which states, "making a report pursuant to article 3 shall not constitute a violation of office confidentiality". Specifically, you asked for guidance concerning the particular persons who would act and how they would proceed according to this provision, while also being attentive to the provisions of art. 3, can. 1548 §2 and article 19 concerning state laws, which in the U.S.A. has mandated reporting, while at the same time has penalties for violations of professional confidentiality.

After review of the matter, I am pleased to inform you of the following observations. As you are already aware, paragraph 1 of art. 4 makes reference to art. 3 which concerns the need to report when there are well-founded motives that merit reporting. Art. 3 of the m.p. obliges that a report be made if there is suspicion of crime of sexual abuse, without prejudice to can. 1548 52 of the 1983 CIC.

Article 4 exempts those who report from office confidentiality, which is imposed by canon law. Consequently, it cannot be said that those who have the duty to report is violating office confidentiality, which according to the law of the church he was required to keep.

---

[1] That document can be found in this issue on page 54.

Regarding the question on who has to make the report, you may find the answer in 52 of art. 3: any person can submit a report concerning the conduct referred to in art. 1.

To be clear, it is always important to make the distinction between canon law and civil law. Paragraph 1 of art. 4 makes reference to canon law and not civil law. The challenge is to reconcile the requirements of canon law with civil law. Depending on the civil legislation of each country (in this case the USA), art. 19 of the m.p. states, "these norms apply without prejudice to the rights and obligations established in each place by state laws". Therefore, one must follow the norms of the m.p. when making the report, taking into consideration the norms in the civil forum and the general moral obligations.

I hope the above information is useful to you. With sentiments of personal esteem and prayerful best wishes, I remain,

Sincerely yours in Christ,
✠Juan Ignacio Arrieta
Secretary

Monsignor Markus Graulich
Under-Secretary

OTHER VATICAN
DOCUMENTS

APOSTOLIC LETTER ISSUED *MOTU PROPRIO*

FOR THE CHANGE OF THE NAME OF THE
VATICAN SECRET ARCHIVE

TO THE

VATICAN APOSTOLIC ARCHIVE

Historical experience teaches us that every human institution, created with the best protection and with vigorous and well-founded hopes for progress, fatally touched by time, precisely to remain faithful to itself and to the ideal aims of its nature, feels the need, not to change its features, but to transpose its inspirational values into different eras and cultures and to make those updates that become convenient and sometimes necessary.

Even the Vatican Secret Archives, for which the Roman Pontiffs have always reserved solicitude and care on account of the immense and important documentary heritage that it preserves, so precious for the Catholic Church as well as for universal culture, cannot escape such inevitable conditioning, in its now more than four centuries-long history.

The Pontifical Archive, which arose from the documentary nucleus of the Apostolic Chamber and of the Apostolic Library itself (the so-called *Bibliotheca secreta*) between the first and second decade of the 17th century, began to be called the Secret (*Archivum Secretum Vaticanum*) only around the middle of that cen. It was accommodated in suitable rooms in the Apostolic Palace, grew over time to a remarkable extent and was immediately opened to requests for documents that came to the Roman Pontiff, to the cardinal Camerlengo and then to the cardinal Archivist and Librarian from all over Europe and the world. While it is true that the official opening of the Archive to researchers from every country was only in 1881, it is also true that between the 17th and 19th centuries many scholarly works could be published with the help of faithful or authentic documentary copies that historians obtained from the custodians and prefects of the Vatican Secret Archive. So much so that the famous German philosopher and mathematician Gottfried Wilhelm von Leibniz, who also drew from it, wrote in 1702 that it could be considered in a certain way the Central Archive of Europe (*quod quodam modo totius Europae commune Archivum censeri debet*).

This long service rendered to the Church, to culture and to scholars from all over the world has always earned the Vatican Secret Archives esteem and gratitude, all the more so since Leo XIII's death today, both because of the progressive "opening" of documentation made available for consultation (which from 2 March 2020, by my provision, will extend until the end of the pontificate of Pius XII), and because of the increase in the number of researchers who are admitted daily to the Archives and helped in every way in their research.

This worthy ecclesial and cultural service, greatly appreciated, responds well to the intentions of all my predecessors, who according to the times and possibilities have favoured historical research in this vast Archive, equipping it, according to the suggestions of cardinal archivists or prefects *pro tempore*, with staff, resources and also with new technologies. In this way the structure of the Archive itself has gradually grown in view of its ever more demanding service to the Church and to the world of culture, always remaining faithful to the teachings and directives of the Popes.

However, there is one aspect that I think could still be useful to update, reaffirming the ecclesial and cultural aims of the mission of the Archives. This aspect concerns the very name of the institute: *Vatican Secret Archive*.

Born, as mentioned, from the *Bibliotheca secreta* del Romano Pontefice, that is, from the part of codes and scriptures more particularly owned and under the direct jurisdiction of the Pope, the Archive was entitled first simply *Archivum novum*, then *Archivum Apostolicum*, then *Archivum Secretum* (the first attestations of the term date back to about 1646).

The term *Secretum*, which has become the institution's proper name and which has prevailed in recent centuries, was justified because it indicated that the new Archive, created at the behest of my predecessor Paul V around 1610-1612, was none other than the Pope's private, separate, reserved archive. This is how all the Popes always intended to define it, and this is how scholars still define it today, without any difficulty. This definition, moreover, was widespread, with similar meaning, in the courts of kings and princes, whose archives were defined indeed as *secret*.

As long as there was still an awareness of the close link between the Latin language and the languages that derive from it, there was no need to explain or even justify this title of *Archivum Secretum*. With the progressive semantic changes that have however occurred in modern languages and in the cultures and social sensibilities of different nations, to a greater or lesser extent, the term *Secretum* in relation to the Vatican Archive began to be misunderstood, to be coloured with ambiguous, even negative nuances. Having lost the true meaning of the term *secretum* and instinctively associating its value with the concept expressed by the modern word "secret", in some areas and environments, even

50

those of a certain cultural importance, this term has taken on the prejudicial meaning of secret, as in not to be revealed and reserved for a few. This is entirely the opposite of what the Vatican Secret Archive has always been and intends to be, which – as my holy predecessor Paul VI said – preserves "echoes and vestiges" of the passage of the Lord in history (Teachings of Paul VI, I, 1963, p. 614). And the Church "is not afraid of history but, rather, she loves it, and would like to love it more and better, as God loves it!" (*Address to the Officials of the Vatican Secret Archives*, 4 March 2019: *L'Osservatore Romano*, 4-5 March 2019, p. 6).

Requested in recent years by some esteemed prelates, as well as by my closest collaborators, and having also listened to the opinion of the Superiors of the same Vatican Secret Archive, with this my *Motu proprio* I decide that:

From now on the present Vatican Secret Archive, without prejudice to its identity, its structure and its mission, should be called the Vatican Apostolic Archive.

Reaffirming its active desire to serve the Church and culture, the new name highlights the close link between the Roman See and the Archive, an indispensable instrument of the Petrine ministry, and at the same time underlines its immediate dependence on the Roman Pontiff, as is already the case in parallel for the name of the Vatican Apostolic Library.

I order that this Apostolic Letter in the form of a *Motu proprio* be promulgated by publication in the daily newspaper *L'Osservatore Romano*, coming into immediate force upon publication, so as to be immediately incorporated into the official documents of the Holy See, and that, subsequently, it be inserted into the *Acta Apostolicae Sedis*.

Given in Rome, at Saint Peter's, on 22 October 2019, seventh of our Pontificate.

FRANCISCUS

Apostolic Letter Issued *Motu Proprio*

by the Supreme Pontiff

Francis

Regarding the Office of Dean of the College of Cardinals

Throughout the centuries the Roman Pontiffs have adapted to the needs of their times the composition of the College of Cardinal Fathers, specially called to undertake the election of the Supreme Pastor of the Church and to assist him in treating issues of the greatest relevance in the daily care of the universal Church.

The Holy Father Paul VI, of eternal memory, with the Motu Proprio of 11 February 1965, expanded the composition of the aforementioned College of Cardinal Fathers, calling to be part of the Order of Bishops, in addition to the Titulars of the suburbicarian Sees of Rome, also those Oriental Patriarchs who had been elevated to the dignity of cardinal (cf. Ad *Purpuratorum Patrum Collegium, AAS* 57 [1965] 295-296).

With the Rescript *ex Audientia* of 26 June 2018, I too took steps to broaden the composition of the members of the aforementioned Order of Bishops, including within it a number of Cardinals who are heads of Roman Dicasteries and equating them in every respect with Cardinals who are assigned a suburbicarian Church and with the Oriental Patriarchs ascribed to the same Order.

In this regard, the regulations of the Church, with clear and precise prescriptions, have for some time now also wisely provided for the singular place, within the College of Cardinals, that belongs to the Cardinal Dean, and in his place, to the Sub-Dean, called to exercise among the brother Cardinals a fraternal and fruitful presidency of primacy *inter pares* (cf. can. 352 § 1). These norms also prescribe the manner of their election by the Brothers who are members of the Episcopal Order (cf. can. 350 § 1 and 352 § 2-3).

Now, however, having accepted the resignation from the office of Dean of the College of Cardinals presented by His Eminence Cardinal Angelo Sodano, whom I thank most sincerely for the high service he has rendered to the College of Cardinals during the almost fifteen years of his mandate, and also having regard to the fact that with the increase in the number of Cardinals, ever greater commitments are being placed on the person of the Cardinal Dean, it seemed opportune to me that from now on the Cardinal Dean, who will continue to be elected from among the members of the Order of Bishops in the manner established by can. 352 § 2 of the Code of Canon Law, remain in office for a five-year period, renewable if necessary, and at the end of his service, he may assume the title of Dean Emeritus of the College of Cardinals.

To all the members of the College of Cardinals of the Holy Roman Church I wish, finally, to express my deep gratitude for their generous service to the Church and to my ministry as Successor of Peter, with my Apostolic Blessing.

Given in Rome, at Saint Peter's, on 29 November of the Year of the Lord 2019, the seventh of our Pontificate.

FRANCISCUS

CONGREGATION FOR THE DOCTRINE OF THE FAITH

RESCRIPTUM EX AUDIENTIA SS.MI

His Holiness Pope Francis, in the Audience granted to the undersigned Cardinal Secretary of State and the undersigned Cardinal Prefect of the Congregation for the Doctrine of the Faith on 4 October 2019, has decided to introduce the following amendments to the *"Normae de gravioribus delictis"* reserved to the judgement of the Congregation for the Doctrine of the Faith, in accordance with the *Motu proprio* of Saint John Paul II *"Sacramentorum Sanctitatis Tutela"* (30 April 2001), as amended by the *Rescriptum ex Audientia SS.mi* dated 21 May 2010 and signed by the then-Prefect of the Congregation for the Doctrine of the Faith, Cardinal William Levada:

Article 1

Art. 6 § 1, 2° *Sacramentorum Sanctitatis Tutela* is replaced in its entirety by the following text:

"The acquisition, possession or distribution by a cleric of pornographic images of minors under the age of eighteen, for purposes of sexual gratification, by whatever means or using whatever technology".

Article 2

§ 1 – Art. 13 *Sacramentorum Sanctitatis Tutela* is replaced in its entirety by the following text:

"The role of Advocate or Procurator is carried out by a member of the faithful possessing a doctorate in canon law, who is approved by the presiding judge of the college".

§ 2 – Art. 14 *Sacramentorum Sanctitatis Tutela* is replaced in its entirety by the following text:

"In other Tribunals, for the cases under these norms, only priests can validly carry out the functions of Judge, Promoter of Justice and Notary".

The Holy Father has ordered that the present *Rescriptum* be published in *L'Osservatore Romano* and in *Acta Apostolicae Sedis*, and take effect on 1 January 2020.

From the Vatican, 3 December 2019

CARDINAL PIETRO PAROLIN
Secretary of State

CARDINAL LUIS FRANCISCO LADARIA
*Prefect of the Congregation
for the Doctrine of the Faith*

SECRETARY OF STATE

RESCRIPTUM EX AUDIENTIA SS.MI

His Holiness Pope Francis, in the Audience granted to His Excellency Archbishop Edgar Peña Parra, Substitute for General Affairs of the Secretariat of State, on 4 December 2019, has decided to issue the Instruction *On the Confidentiality of Legal Proceedings*, attached to the present *Rescriptum*, of which it forms an integral part.

The Holy Father has determined that the *Rescriptum* shall have firm and stable application, notwithstanding anything to the contrary, even if worthy of special mention, that it shall be promulgated by publication in *L'Osservatore Romano*, with immediate force, and then be published in the official commentary *Acta Apostolicae Sedis*.

From the Vatican, 6 December 2019

CARDINAL PIETRO PAROLIN
Secretary of State

INSTRUCTION
On the Confidentiality of Legal Proceedings

1. The pontifical secret does not apply to accusations, trials and decisions involving the offences referred to in:

a) Article 1 of the *Motu proprio "Vos estis lux mundi"* (7 May 2019);

b) Article 6 of the *Normae de gravioribus delictis* reserved to the judgement of the Congregation for the Doctrine of the Faith, in accordance with the *Motu proprio "Sacramentorum Sanctitatis Tutela"* of Saint John Paul II (30 April 2001), and subsequent amendments.

2. Nor does the pontifical secret apply when such offenses were committed in conjunction with other offences.

3. In the cases referred to in No. 1, the information is to be treated in such a way as to ensure its security, integrity and confidentiality in accordance with the prescriptions of canons 471, 2° CIC and 244 §2, 2° CCEO, for the sake of protecting the good name, image and privacy of all persons involved.

4. Office confidentiality shall not prevent the fulfilment of the obligations laid down in all places by civil laws, including any reporting obligations, and the execution of enforceable requests of civil judicial authorities.

5. The person who files the report, the person who alleges to have been harmed and the witnesses shall not be bound by any obligation of silence with regard to matters involving the case.

Address of His Holiness Pope Francis
to Participants in the Plenary Assembly
of the Pontifical Council for Legislative Texts

Consistory Hall
Friday, 21 February 2020

Mister Cardinals,
Dear brothers in the episcopate and in the priesthood,
Dear brothers and sisters!

I am pleased to welcome you today for the first time, at the end of your plenary session. I thank the President for recalling the spirit in which your work was conducted, which had as its subject the outline of the revision of Book VI of the Code of Canon Law, *De sanctionibus in Ecclesia*. This meeting gives me the opportunity to thank you for your service which, in the name and with the authority of the Successor of Peter, you perform for the benefit of the Churches and Pastors (cf. *Christus Dominus*, 9). The specific collaboration of your Dicastery is defined in the Constitution *Pastor Bonus* (cf. Articles 154-158), which summarises it as assistance to the legislative function of the Supreme Pontiff, the universal Legislator, the correct interpretation of the laws enacted by him, assistance to other Dicasteries in matters of canon law, and the supervision of the legitimacy of normative texts enacted by legislators under the supreme authority.

The Pontifical Council for Legislative Texts, through various initiatives, also undertakes to offer its help to the Pastors of the particular Churches and the episcopal conferences for the correct interpretation and application of the law; more generally, in disseminating knowledge of and attention to it. It is necessary to re-acquire and deepen the true meaning of law in the Church, the Mystical Body of Christ, where the preeminence is of the Word of God and the Sacraments, while the juridical norm has a necessary but subordinate role in the service of communion. In this regard it is opportune that the Dicastery should help to make people reflect on a genuine legal formation in the Church, enabling an understanding the pastoral nature of canon law, its instrumentality with regard to the *salus animarum* (can. 1752), and its necessity for obedience to the virtue of justice, which must always be affirmed and guaranteed.

From this perspective, Benedict XVI's invitation in his *Letter to Seminarians* is very timely, and valid for all the faithful: "Learn to understand and - dare I say it - to love canon law, appreciating how necessary it is and valuing its practical applications: a society without law would be a society without rights. Law is the condition of love" (5). Making the laws of the Church known and applying them is not a hindrance to the presumed pastoral "effectiveness" of those who want to solve problems without law, but rather a guarantee of the search for solutions that are not arbitrary, but instead truly just and, therefore, truly pastoral. By avoiding arbitrary solutions, the law becomes a valid bulwark in defence of the least and the poor, a protective shield for those who risk falling victim to the powerful. We see today in this context of piecemeal world war, we see the lack of law, always. Dictatorships are born and grow without law. In the Church this cannot happen.

The theme under study in your Plenary also follows in this direction, to point out that criminal law is also a pastoral instrument and as such must be considered and accepted. The bishop must be increasingly aware that in his Church, of which he is constituted as pastor and head, he is therefore also a judge among the faithful entrusted to him. But the role of judge always has a pastoral imprint in as much as it aims at communion among the members of the People of God. This is what is prescribed in the current Code: when the Ordinary has ascertained that by other means dictated by pastoral concern it has not been possible to obtain sufficient reparation for an injustice, the restoration of justice, the amendment of the offender, only then must he initiate the judicial or administrative procedure to inflict or declare the penalties appropriate for the purpose (cf. can. 1341). From this it can be deduced that the criminal sanction is always the *extrema ratio*, the extreme remedy to which recourse is made when all other possible ways of achieving regulatory compliance have proved ineffective.

In contrast to what is provided for by the State legislature, canonical punishment always has a pastoral significance and pursues not only a function of respect for the law, but also reparation and above all the good of the guilty person himself. The aim of reparation is to restore, as far as possible, the conditions preceding the violation which disturbed communion. Indeed, every crime affects the whole of the Church, whose communion has been violated by those who deliberately attack it with their own behaviour. The aim of the recovery of the individual emphasises that canonical punishment is not a merely coercive instrument, but instead has a distinctly medicinal character. Ultimately, it represents a positive means for the realisation of the Kingdom, for rebuilding justice in the community of the faithful, who are called to personal and common sanctification.

The task of revising Book VI of the Latin Code, in which you have been engaged for some years and which reaches a conclusion with this Plenary, moves in the right direction: to update the criminal law to render it more organic and in conformity with the new situations and problems of the current socio-cultural context, and at the same time to offer suitable tools to facilitate its application. I urge you to continue with tenacity in this task. I pray for this and bless all of you and your work. And please do not forget to pray for me, because I too must be a judge. Thank you.[1]

[1] Available on the Vatican website at http://www.vatican.va/content/francesco/en/speeches/2020/february/documents/papa-francesco_20200221_testi-legislativi.html (accessed on 1 October 2020).

ADDRESS OF HIS HOLINESS POPE FRANCIS
TO THE OFFICIALS OF THE TRIBUNAL OF THE ROMAN ROTA
FOR THE INAUGURATION OF THE JUDICIAL YEAR

Clementine Hall
Saturday, 25 January 2020[1]

Your Excellency,

Prelate Auditors,

Dear Officials of the Roman Rota,

I am pleased to be able to meet you today, on the occasion of the inauguration of the New Judicial Year of this Tribunal. I warmly thank His Excellency, the Dean, for the noble words he addressed to me and for the wise methodological resolutions that have been formulated.

I wish to return to the catechesis of the General Audience of Wednesday, 13 November 2019, offering to you today a further reflection on the primary role the spouses Aquila and Priscilla played as examples of married life. Indeed, in order to follow Jesus, the Church has to work according to three conditions validated by the Divine Teacher himself: *itinerancy*, *promptness* and *decision* (cf. Angelus, 30 June 2019). The Church is, by her very nature, on the move; she does not remain confined and unperturbed in her specific area; she is open to the widest horizons. The Church is sent forth to take the Gospel to the streets and to reach the human and existential peripheries. It reminds us of the New Testament married couple, Aquila and Priscilla.

The Holy Spirit wished to place this admirable example of *itinerant* spouses beside the Apostle [Paul]. Indeed both in the Acts of the Apostles and according to Paul's description, they were never still but always in continuous movement. And we wonder, why for many centuries, this example of itinerant spouses did not have their identity recognized as evangelizing spouses within the pastoral teaching of the Church. It is what our parish Churches need, in particular in urban areas where the parish priest and his assistants in the clergy will never have enough time and energy to reach the faithful who, while calling themselves

---

[1] Available on the Vatican website at http://w2.vatican.va/content/francesco/en/ speeches/2020/january/documents/papa-francesco_20200125_rota-romana.html (accessed on 30 September 2020).

Christian, do not receive the Sacraments and are without or almost without the knowledge of Christ.

So many centuries later, the *modern image* of these holy spouses ever on the move so that Jesus might be known, is surprising: They evangelized, transmitting their passion for the Lord and for the Gospel, a passion of the heart that translated into practical gestures of proximity, of closeness to the neediest brothers and sisters, of welcome and care.

In the *preface* to the reform of the Marriage Process, I was insistent on two pearls: proximity and gratuity. This should not be forgotten. Saint Paul found in this couple a way to be *close* to the distant ones and he loved them and stayed with them in Corinth for more than one year, because they were spouses who were teachers of selflessness. I often feel afraid of the judgement that God will have for us over these two things. In judging, was I close to the heart of the people? In judging, did I open my heart to *gratuity* or was I taken up by commercial interests? God's judgment will be quite harsh on this.

From Aquila and Priscilla, Christian spouses should learn how to fall in love with Christ and to be close to families, who often lack the light of faith, not through their own fault, but because they are left on the sidelines by our pastoral care: an elite pastoral care that forgets the people.

How I would like this discourse not to be simply a symphony of words but rather that it may spur pastors, bishops, and parish priests to seek to love, as the Apostle Paul did, spouses as humble missionaries willing to reach our cities' squares and buildings where the Gospel's light and the voice of Jesus fail to penetrate. And at the same time, Christian spouses who have the courage to awaken others from their slumber, as Aquila and Priscilla did, capable of being agents, let us not say autonomously, but certainly filled with enough courage, to awaken from lethargy and slumber, those pastors who perhaps are stuck in the philosophy of the small circle of perfects. The Lord came to seek the sinners not the perfect ones.

In the Encyclical Letter *Ecclesiam Suam* Saint Paul VI observed: "before speaking, we must take great care to listen not only to what men say, but more especially to what they have it in their hearts to say. Only then will we understand them and respect them, and even, as far as possible, agree with them" (n. 87). Listening to the heart of mankind.

As I recommended to Italian Bishops, it is a case of listening to the flock, being "close to the people, attentive to learning their language, to draw near to each person with charity, supporting people in the nights of their solitude, restlessness and failures" (Discourse to the General Assembly of the Episcopal Conference of Italy, 19 May 2014).

We must be aware that it is not the pastors who, through their human enterprise—albeit in good will—invent holy Christian couples. They are the work of the Holy Spirit who is always the protagonist of the mission, and they are already present in our territorial communities. It is up to us pastors to illuminate them, to give them visibility, to make them wellsprings of a new ability to live a Christian marriage, and also to protect them so they do not fall into ideologies. These couples that the Holy Spirit certainly continues to enliven must be ready "to go out of themselves and be open to others, to live the closeness, the way of living together, which transforms every interpersonal relationship into an experience of fraternity" (General Audience, 16 October 2019). Let us think about pastoral care as a catechumenate before and after marriage. These are the couples that should do it and move forward.

It is necessary to be vigilant so that they do not fall into the danger of particularism, opting to live in chosen groups. On the contrary, it is necessary "to open to the universality of salvation" (ibid.). Indeed if we are grateful to God for the presence within the Church of movements and associations that do not neglect the formation of Christian spouses, then we must firmly state that the parish is the ecclesial place for proclamation and witness because it is in that territorial context that Christian spouses worthy of shedding light already dwell. They can be active witnesses of conjugal and family beauty and love (cf. Apostolic Exhortation *Amoris Laetitia*, 126-130).

Thus the Apostolic Action of the parish is illuminated in the Church by the presence of spouses like those described by Paul and Luke in the New Testament; never still, always on the move, certainly with children, according to what the iconography of the Oriental Churches has handed down to us. Therefore, may pastors allow themselves to be illuminated by the Spirit today too, so that this salvific news may be fulfilled by couples who are often already prepared, but *not called*. They exist.

The Church today needs married couples *on the move* anywhere in the world. Ideally starting, however, from the roots of the Church of the first four centuries and that is from the catacombs, as Saint Paul VI did at the end of the Council by going to the Catacombs of Domitilla. In those catacombs that saintly Pontiff said: Here, Christianity planted its roots in poverty, in the ostracism of the powers, in the suffering of unjust and bloody persecutions. Here, the Church was stripped of all human power, she was poor, she was humble, she was pious, she was oppressed, she was heroic. Here, the primacy of the Spirit of which the Gospel speaks had its dark, almost mysterious but undefeated affirmation, his incomparable witness, his martyrdom (cf. Homily, 12 September 1965).

If the Spirit is not invoked and thus remains unknown and absent (cf. Homily, *Santa Marta*, 9 May 2016) in the context of our particular Churches, we will lack the strength of those Christian married couples who are the soul and the form of evangelization. In practice: living the parish as that "juridical-salvific" territory because it is "home among homes", families of families (cf. homily at Albano), 21 September 2019); a Church — that is a parish — poor for the poor; enthusiastic couples in love with their faith in the Risen One, capable of a new revolution of the tenderness of love like Aquila and Priscilla, who never felt satisfied or inadequate.

One might think that these holy spouses of the New Testament never had the time to appear tired. This is actually how they were described by Paul and Luke for whom they were almost indispensable companions precisely because they were not called by Paul but created by the Spirit of Jesus. It is here that their apostolic dignity as Christian spouses is founded. It is the Holy Spirit who created them. Let us think about when a missionary arrives in a place: the Holy Spirit is already there waiting for him. The long silence surrounding these holy figures of the early Church is certainly quite perplexing.

I invite and urge all the brother bishops and pastors to indicate these saintly spouses of the early Church as faithful and bright companions of the Pastors of that time; as support, today of, for example, how young and elderly Christian married couples can always make Christian marriage fruitful with children in Christ. We must be convinced, and I would like to say certain, that similar married couples in the Church are already a gift of God, and not through our merit, but because they are the fruit of the action of the Spirit that never abandons the Church. Rather, the Spirit awaits the ardour of our pastors so that the light that these spouses radiate in the peripheries of the world are not extinguished. (cf. *Gaudium et Spes*, nn.4-10).

Hence, allow the Spirit to renew us so as not to resign ourselves to being a Church of the few, to almost enjoy being isolated leaven lacking the capacity of the spouses of the New Testament, to multiply in humility and obedience to the Spirit. The Spirit that illuminates and is capable of making salvific our human action and our very poverty; it is capable of making salvific all our activities; ever convinced that the Church does not grow by proselytism but by attraction — the witness of these people attracts — and always ensuring the signature of bearing witness.

We do not know whether or not Aquila and Priscilla died as martyrs but they certainly are a sign of martyrdom, at least spiritually for today's spouses, that is, witnesses capable of being leaven in the flour, of being leaven in the dough, [leaven] that dies to become the mass of dough (cf. Discourse to the Associations of Catholic Families in Europe, 1 June 2017). This is possible everywhere today.

Dear Judges of the Roman Rota, the *darkness of faith* or the *desert of faith* that your decisions, starting 20 years ago, have stated as possible causes for the annulment of consent, gives me, as it did to my predecessor Benedict XVI (cf. Allocutions of the Roman Rota, 23 January 2015 and 22 January 2016; 22 January 2011; cf. art. 14, *Ratio procedendi* of the Motu Proprio *Mitis Iudex Dominus Iesus*), the reason to extend a serious and pressing invitation to the children of the Church of our time, to all feel called to deliver to the future, the beauty of the Christian family.

The Church needs *ubicumque terrarum* of married couples like Aquila and Priscilla who can speak and live with the *authority* of Baptism, that "does not consist in commanding and making oneself heard, but in being consistent, being a witness and for this reason, being companions on the way of the Lord" (Homily, *Santa Marta*, 14 January 2020).

I give thanks to the Lord because still today he gives the children of the Church the courage and the light to return to the beginnings of faith and find again the passion of the spouses Aquila and Priscilla, so that they may be recognizable in every marriage celebrated in Christ Jesus.

NOTE FROM THE APOSTOLIC PENITENTIARY ON THE SACRAMENT OF RECONCILIATION IN THE CURRENT PANDEMIC

«I am with you always»

(Mt 28: 20)

The gravity of the present circumstances calls for reflection on the urgency and centrality of the Sacrament of Reconciliation, together with some necessary clarifications, both for the lay faithful and for ministers called to celebrate the Sacrament.

Even in the time of COVID-19, the Sacrament of Reconciliation is administered in accordance with universal canon law and with the provisions of the *Ordo Paenitentiae*.

Individual confession is the ordinary way of celebrating this sacrament (cf. can. 960 *CIC*), while collective absolution, without prior individual confession, cannot be imparted except where there is an imminent danger of death, since there is not enough time to hear the confessions of individual penitents (cf. c. 961 §1 *CIC*), or a grave necessity (cf. c. 961 §2 *CIC*), the consideration of which is the responsibility of the diocesan bishop, taking into account the criteria agreed upon with the other members of the Episcopal Conference (cf. c. 455 §2 CIC) and without prejudice to the necessity, for valid absolution, of *votum sacramenti* on the part of the individual penitent, that is to say, the purpose of confessing serious sins in due time, which at the time could not be confessed (cf. c. 962, §1 CIC).

This Apostolic Penitentiary believes that, especially in the places most affected by the pandemic contagion and until the phenomenon recedes, the cases of serious need mentioned in can. 961, § 2 CIC above mentioned, will occur.

Any further specification is delegated by law to diocesan bishops, always taking into account the supreme good of the salvation of souls (cf. c. 1752 CIC).

Should there arise a sudden need to impart sacramental absolution to several faithful together, the priest is obliged to warn the diocesan bishop as far as possible or, if he cannot, to inform him as soon as possible (cf. *Ordo Paenitentiae*, n. 32).

In the present pandemic emergency, it is therefore up to the diocesan bishop to indicate to priests and penitents the prudent attentions to be adopted in the individual celebration of sacramental reconciliation, such as the celebration in a ventilated place outside the confessional, the adoption of a suitable distance, the use of protective masks, without prejudice to absolute attention to the safeguarding of the sacramental seal and the necessary discretion.

Furthermore, it is always up to the diocesan bishop to determine, in the territory of his own ecclesiastical circumscription and with regard to the level of pandemic contagion, the cases of grave necessity in which it is lawful to impart collective absolution: for example, at the entrance to hospital wards, where the infected faithful in danger of death are hospitalised, using as far as possible and with the appropriate precautions the means of amplifying the voice so that absolution may be heard.

Consideration should be given to the need and advisability of setting up, where necessary, in agreement with the health authorities, groups of "extraordinary hospital chaplains", also on a voluntary basis and in compliance with the norms of protection from contagion, to guarantee the necessary spiritual assistance to the sick and dying.

Where the individual faithful find themselves in the painful impossibility of receiving sacramental absolution, it should be remembered that perfect contrition, coming from the love of God, beloved above all things, expressed by a sincere request for forgiveness (that which the penitent is at present able to express) and accompanied by *votum confessionis*, that is, by the firm resolution to have recourse, as soon as possible, to sacramental confession, obtains forgiveness of sins, even mortal ones (cf. CCC, no. 1452).

Never before has the Church experienced thus the power of the communion of saints, raising to her Crucified and Risen Lord her vows and prayers, especially the Sacrifice of Holy Mass, celebrated daily, even without the presence of the people, by priests.

Like a good mother, the Church implores the Lord that humanity may be freed from such a scourge, invoking the intercession of the Blessed Virgin Mary, Mother of Mercy and Health of the Sick, and of her Spouse Saint Joseph, under whose patronage the Church has always walked the world.

May Mary Most Holy and Saint Joseph obtain for us abundant graces of reconciliation and salvation, in attentive listening to the Word of the Lord, which he repeats to humanity today: "Be still and know that I am God" (Ps 46: 10), "I am with you always" (Mt 28 :20).

Given in Rome, from the seat of the Apostolic Penitentiary, on March 19, 2020,

Solemnity of St. Joseph, Spouse of the Blessed Virgin Mary, Patron of the Universal Church.

Mauro Cardinal Piacenza
Major Penitentiary

Krzysztof Nykiel
Regent

CONGREGATION FOR CLERGY

ON ALIENATION AND BANKRUPTCY PROCEEDINGS

From the Vatican, 15 June 2020

Prot. N.

Your Excellency,

I am writing pursuant to the competence of this Dicastery in matters pertaining to the correct administration of ecclesiastical temporal goods, as found in the Apostolic Constitution *Pastor Bonus*, article 98.

In recent months, the Congregation has received news of the declaration of bankruptcy by several diocesan Bishops in the United States, acting on behalf of the juridic persons whose legal representatives they are (cf. CIC can. 393). In most of these cases, the permission of the Holy See was sought, in conformity to the prescripts of law. In some, however, the necessary permission was not requested.

Therefore, I would ask Your Excellency kindly to remind the Most Reverend Ordinaries of the United States that the declaration of bankruptcy, as a "transaction which can worsen the patrimonial condition of a juridic person" (cf. can. 1295), is subject to the requirements of canon 1292 §2 whenever it is foreseen that the legal proceedings could involve the alienation of temporal goods whose value exceeds the maximum amounts set by the decree of the United States Conference of Catholic Bishops issued on 1 December 2011.

Thanking Your Excellency for this gracious assistance, I am,

Sincerely yours in Christ,

✠Beniamino Cardinal Stella
Prefect

CONGREGATION FOR THE DOCTRINE OF THE FAITH

VADEMECUM

ON CERTAIN POINTS OF PROCEDURE IN TREATING CASES OF SEXUAL ABUSE OF MINORS COMMITTED BY CLERICS

Version 1.0

of 16 July 2020

NOTA BENE:

a. In addition to the delicts listed in art. 6 of the *Normae* promulgated by the Motu Proprio *Sacramentorum Sanctitatis Tutela*, what follows is to be observed – with eventual adaptations – in all cases involving delicts reserved to the Congregation for the Doctrine of the Faith;

b. The following abbreviations will be used: CIC: *Codex Iuris Canonici*; CCEO: *Codex Canonum Ecclesiarum Orientalium*; SST: Motu Proprio *Sacramentorum Sanctitatis Tutela* – 2010 Revised Norms; VELM: Motu Proprio *Vos Estis Lux Mundi* – 2019; CDF: *Congregatio pro Doctrina Fidei*.

* * *

0. Introduction

In response to numerous questions about the procedures to be followed in those penal cases for which it is competent, the Congregation for the Doctrine of the Faith has prepared this *Vademecum*, intended primarily for Ordinaries and other personnel needing to apply the canonical norms governing cases of the sexual abuse of minors by clerics.

The present manual is meant to serve as a handbook for those charged with ascertaining the truth in such criminal cases, leading them step-by-step from the *notitia criminis* to the definitive conclusion of the case.

While not issuing new norms or altering current canonical legislation, this manual seeks to clarify the various stages of the procedures involved. Its use is to be encouraged, since a standardized praxis will contribute to a better administration of justice.

Reference is made above all to the two Codes presently in force (CIC and CCEO); the *Norms on Delicts Reserved to the Congregation for the Doctrine of the Faith* in the revised 2010 version, issued with the Motu Proprio *Sacramentorum Sanctitatis Tutela*, taking account of the revisions introduced by the *Rescripta ex Audientia* of 3 and 6 December 2019; the Motu Proprio *Vos Estis Lux Mundi*; and, not least, the praxis of the Congregation for the Doctrine of the Faith, which has in recent years become increasingly clear and consolidated.

Intended to be flexible, this manual can be periodically updated if the norms to which it refers are modified, or if the praxis of the Congregation calls for further clarifications and revisions.

A choice was made not to include in this *Vademecum* guidelines for carrying out the judicial penal process in the first grade of judgment, since it was felt that the procedure set forth in the present Codes is sufficiently clear and detailed.

It is hoped that this handbook will assist Dioceses, Institutes of Consecrated Life and Societies of Apostolic Life, Episcopal Conferences and the various ecclesiastical circumscriptions to better understand and implement the requirements of justice regarding a *delictum gravius* that constitutes for the whole Church a profound and painful wound that cries out for healing.

I. What constitutes the delict?

1. The delict in question includes every external offense against the sixth commandment of the Decalogue committed by a cleric with a minor (cf. c. 1395 §2 CIC; art. 6 §1, 1° SST).

2. The typology of the delict is quite broad; it can include, for example, sexual relations (consensual or non-consensual), physical contact for sexual gratification, exhibitionism, masturbation, the production of pornography, inducement to prostitution, conversations and/or propositions of a sexual nature, which can also occur through various means of communication.

3. The concept of "minor" in these cases has varied over the course of time. Prior to 30 April 2001, a minor was defined as a person under 16 years of age (even though in some particular legislations – for example in the United States [from 1994] and Ireland [from 1996] – the age had already been raised to 18). After 30 April 2001, with the promulgation of the Motu Proprio *Sacramentorum Sanctitatis Tutela*, the age was universally raised to 18 years, and this is the age currently in effect. These variations must be taken into account when determining whether the "minor" in question was in fact such, according to the legal definition in effect at the time of the facts.

4. The use of the term "minor" does not reflect the distinction occasionally proposed by the psychological sciences between acts of "paedophilia" and those of "ephebophilia", that is, involving post-pubescent adolescents. Their degree of sexual maturity does not affect the canonical definition of the delict.

5. The revision of the Motu Proprio SST, promulgated on 21 May 2010, states that a person who habitually has the imperfect use of reason is to be considered equivalent to a minor (cf. art. 6 §1, 1° SST). With regard to the use of the term "vulnerable adult", elsewhere described as "any person in a state of infirmity, physical or mental deficiency, or deprivation of personal liberty which, in fact, even occasionally limits their ability to understand or to want or otherwise resist the offence" (cf. art. 1 §2, b VELM), it should be noted that this definition includes other situations than those pertaining to the competence of the CDF, which remains limited to minors under eighteen years of age and to those who "habitually have an imperfect use of reason". Other situations outside of these cases are handled by the competent Dicasteries (cf. art. 7 §1 VELM).

6. SST has also introduced (cf. art. 6 §1, 2° SST) three new delicts involving minors, i.e., the acquisition, possession (even temporary) or distribution by a cleric of pornographic images of minors under the age of 14 (as of 1 January 2020, under the age of 18) for purposes of sexual gratification by whatever means or using whatever technology. From 1 June to 31 December 2019, the acquisition, possession, or distribution of pornographic material involving minors between 14 and 18 years of age by clerics or by members of Institutes of Consecrated Life or Societies of Apostolic Life are delicts for which other Dicasteries are competent (cf. arts. 1 and 7 VELM). From 1 January 2020, the CDF is competent for these delicts if committed by clerics.

7. It should be noted that these three delicts can be addressed canonically only after the date that SST took effect, namely, 21 May 2010. The production of pornography involving minors, on the other hand, falls under the typology of delict listed in nos. 1-4 of the present *Vademecum*, and therefore is also to be dealt with if it occurred prior to that date.

8. In accordance with the law governing religious who are members of the Latin Church (cf. cc. 695ff. CIC), the delict mentioned above in no. 1 can also entail dismissal from a religious Institute. The following should be kept in mind: a/ such dismissal is not a penalty, but rather an administrative act of the supreme Moderator; b/ to issue a decree of dismissal, the relevant procedure described in canons 695 §2, 699 and 700 CIC must be carefully followed; c/ confirmation of the decree of dismissal demanded by canon 700 CIC must be requested from the CDF; d/ dismissal from the Institute entails the loss of membership in the Institute

and the cessation of vows and obligations deriving from profession (cf. c. 701 CIC), as well as the prohibition of exercising any sacred orders received until the conditions referred to in canon 701 CIC are met. The same rules, suitably adapted, are also applicable to definitively incorporated members of Societies of Apostolic Life (cf. c. 746 CIC).

II. What must be done when information is received about a possible delict (*notitia de delicto*)?

a/ What is meant by the term *notitia de delicto*?

9. A *notitia de delicto* (cf. c. 1717 §1 CIC; c. 1468 §1 CCEO; art. 16 SST; art. 3 VELM), occasionally called *notitia criminis*, consists of any information about a possible delict that in any way comes to the attention of the Ordinary or Hierarch. It need not be a formal complaint.

10. This *notitia* can come from a variety of sources: it can be formally presented to the Ordinary or Hierarch, orally or in writing, by the alleged victim, his or her guardians or other persons claiming to have knowledge about the matter; it can become known to the Ordinary or Hierarch through the exercise of his duty for vigilance; it can be reported to the Ordinary or Hierarch by the civil authorities through channels provided for by local legislation; it can be made known through the communications media (including social media); it can come to his knowledge through hearsay, or in any other adequate way.

11. At times, a *notitia de delicto* can derive from an anonymous source, namely, from unidentified or unidentifiable persons. The anonymity of the source should not automatically lead to considering the report as false. Nonetheless, for easily understandable reasons, great caution should be exercised in considering this type of *notitia*, and anonymous reports certainly should not be encouraged.

12. Likewise, when a *notitia de delicto* comes from sources whose credibility might appear at first doubtful, it is not advisable to dismiss the matter *a priori*.

13. At times, a *notitia de delicto* lacks specific details (names, dates, times…). Even if vague and unclear, it should be appropriately assessed and, if reasonably possible, given all due attention.

14. It must be pointed out that a report of a *delictum gravius* received in confession is under placed the strictest bond of the sacramental seal (cf. c. 983 §1 CIC; c. 733 §1 CCEO; art. 4 §1, 5° SST). A confessor who learns of a *delictum gravius* during the celebration of the sacrament should seek to convince the penitent to make that information known by other means, in order to enable the appropriate authorities to take action.

15. The responsibility for vigilance incumbent on the Ordinary or Hierarch does not demand that he constantly monitor the clerics subject to him, yet neither does it allow him to consider himself exempt from keeping informed about their conduct in these areas, especially if he becomes aware of suspicions, scandalous behaviour, or serious misconduct.

b/ What actions should be taken upon receiving a *notitia de delicto*?

16. Art. 16 SST (cf. also cc. 1717 CIC and 1468 CCEO) states that, when a *notitia de delicto* is received, a preliminary investigation ought to ensue, provided that the report is *"saltem verisimilis"*. If that plausibility proves unfounded, there is no need to pursue the *notitia de delicto*, although care should be taken to keep the documentation, together with a written explanation regarding the reasons for the decision.

17. Even in cases where there is no explicit legal obligation to do so, the ecclesiastical authorities should make a report to the competent civil authorities if this is considered necessary to protect the person involved or other minors from the danger of further criminal acts.

18. Given the sensitive nature of the matter (for example, the fact that sins against the sixth commandment of the Decalogue rarely occur in the presence of witnesses), a determination that the *notitia* lacks the semblance of truth (which can lead to omitting the preliminary investigation) will be made only in the case of the manifest impossibility of proceeding according to the norms of canon law. For example, if it turns out that at the time of the delict of which he is accused, the person was not yet a cleric; if it comes to light that the presumed victim was not a minor (on this point, cf. no. 3); if it is a well-known fact that the person accused could not have been present at the place of the delict when the alleged actions took place.

19. Even in these cases, however, it is advisable that the Ordinary or Hierarch communicate to the CDF the *notitia de delicto* and the decision made to forego the preliminary investigation due to the manifest lack of the semblance of truth.

20. Here it should be mentioned that in cases of improper and imprudent conduct, even in the absence of a delict involving minors, should it prove necessary to protect the common good and to avoid scandal, the Ordinary or Hierarch is competent to take other administrative provisions with regard to the person accused (for example, restrictions on his ministry), or to impose the penal remedies mentioned in canon 1339 CIC for the purpose of preventing delicts (cf. c. 1312 §3 CIC) or to give the public reprimand referred to in canon 1427 CCEO.

In the case of delicts that are *non graviora*, the Ordinary or Hierarch should employ the juridical means appropriate to the particular circumstances.

21. According to canon 1717 CIC and canon 1468 CCEO, responsibility for the preliminary investigation belongs to the Ordinary or Hierarch who received the *notitia de delicto*, or to a suitable person selected by him. The eventual omission of this duty could constitute a delict subject to a canonical procedure in conformity with the Code of Canon Law and the Motu Proprio *Come una madre amorevole*, as well as art. 1 §1, b VELM.

22. This task belongs to the Ordinary or Hierarch of the accused cleric or, if different, the Ordinary or Hierarch of the place where the alleged delicts took place. In the latter case, it will naturally be helpful for there to be communication and cooperation between the different Ordinaries involved, in order to avoid conflicts of competence or the duplication of labour, particularly if the cleric is a religious.

23. Should an Ordinary or Hierarch encounter difficulties in initiating or carrying out the preliminary investigation, he should immediately contact the CDF for advice or help in resolving any eventual questions.

24. It can happen that the *notitia de delicto* comes directly to the CDF and not through the Ordinary or Hierarch. In that case, the CDF can ask the latter to carry out the investigations or, in accordance with art. 17 SST, can carry them out itself.

25. The CDF, according to its own judgment, by explicit request or by necessity, can also ask any other Ordinary or Hierarch to carry out the preliminary investigation.

26. The preliminary canonical investigation must be carried out independently of any corresponding investigation by the civil authorities. In those cases where state legislation prohibits investigations parallel to its own, the ecclesiastical authorities should refrain from initiating the preliminary investigation and report the accusation to the CDF, including any useful documentation. In cases where it seems appropriate to await the conclusion of the civil investigations in order to acquire their results, or for other reasons, the Ordinary or Hierarch would do well to seek the advice of the CDF in this regard.

27. The investigation should be carried out with respect for the civil laws of each state (cf. art. 19 VELM).

28. For the delicts considered here, it should be noted that the terms of prescription for the criminal action have varied significantly over time. The terms currently in

effect are defined by art. 7 SST.[1] Yet since art. 7 §1 SST permits the CDF to derogate from prescription in individual cases, an Ordinary or Hierarch who has determined that the times for prescription have elapsed must still respond to the *notitia de delicto* and carry out the eventual preliminary investigation, communicating its results to the CDF, which is competent to decide whether prescription is to be retained or to grant a derogation from it. In forwarding the acts, it would be helpful for the Ordinary or Hierarch to express his personal opinion regarding an eventual derogation, basing it on concrete circumstances (e.g., cleric's health status or age, cleric's ability to exercise right of self-defence, harm caused by the alleged criminal act, scandal given).

29. In these sensitive preliminary acts, the Ordinary or Hierarch can seek the advice of the CDF (as is possible at any time during the handling of a case) and freely consult with experts in canonical penal matters. In the latter case, however, care should be taken to avoid any inappropriate or illicit diffusion of information to the public that could prejudice successive investigations or give the impression that the facts or the guilt of the cleric in question have already been determined with certainty.

30. It should be noted that already in this phase one is bound to observe the secret of office. It must be remembered, however, that an obligation of silence about the allegations cannot be imposed on the one reporting the matter, on a person who claims to have been harmed, and on witnesses.

31. In accordance with art. 2 §3 VELM, an Ordinary who has received a *notitia de delicto* must transmit it immediately to the Ordinary or Hierarch of the place where the events were said to have occurred, as well as to the proper Ordinary or Hierarch of the person reported, namely, in the case of a religious, to his major Superior, if the latter is his proper Ordinary, and in the case of a diocesan priest, to the Ordinary of the diocese or the eparchial Bishop of incardination. In cases where the local Ordinary or Hierarch and the proper Ordinary or Hierarch are not the same person, it is preferable that they contact each other to determine which of them will carry out the investigation. In cases where the report concerns a member of an Institute of Consecrated Life or a Society of Apostolic Life, the

---

[1] Art. 7 SST - §1. A criminal action for delicts reserved to the Congregation for the Doctrine of the Faith is extinguished by prescription after twenty years, with due regard to the right of the Congregation for the Doctrine of the Faith to derogate from prescription in individual cases. §2. Prescription runs according to the norm of canon 1362 §2 of the Code of Canon Law and canon 1152 §3 of the Code of Canons of the Eastern Churches. However in the delict mentioned in art. 6 §1 no. 1, prescription begins to run from the day on which a minor completes his eighteenth year of age.

major Superior will also inform the supreme Moderator and, in the case of Institutes and Societies of diocesan right, also the respective Bishop.

III. How does the preliminary investigation take place?

32. The preliminary investigation takes place in accordance with the criteria and procedures set forth in canon 1717 CIC or canon 1468 CCEO and cited below.

a/ What is the preliminary investigation?

33. It must always be kept in mind that the preliminary investigation is not a trial, nor does it seek to attain moral certitude as to whether the alleged events occurred. It serves: a/ to gather data useful for a more detailed examination of the *notitia de delicto*; and b/ to determine the plausibility of the report, that is, to determine that which is called *fumus delicti*, namely the sufficient basis both in law and in fact so as to consider the accusation as having the semblance of truth.

34. For this reason, as the canons cited in no. 32 indicate, the preliminary investigation should gather detailed information about the *notitia de delicto* with regard to facts, circumstances and imputability. It is not necessary at this phase to assemble complete elements of proof (e.g., testimonies, expert opinions), since this would be the task of an eventual subsequent penal procedure. The important thing is to reconstruct, to the extent possible, the facts on which the accusation is based, the number and time of the criminal acts, the circumstances in which they took place and general details about the alleged victims, together with a preliminary evaluation of the eventual physical, psychological and moral harm inflicted. Care should also be taken care to determine any possible relation to the sacramental internal forum (in this regard, however, account must be taken of the prescriptions of art. 24 SST[2]). At this point, any other delicts attributed to the accused (cf. art. 8 §2 SST[3]) can be added, as well as any indication of problematic facts emerging from his biographical profile. It can be useful to assemble testimonies and documents, of any kind or provenance (including the results of investigations or trials carried out by civil authorities), which may in fact prove helpful for substantiating and validating the plausibility of the accusation. It is likewise possible at this point to indicate eventual exempting, mitigating or

---

[2] Art. 24 SST - §1. In cases concerning the delicts mentioned in art. 4 §1, the Tribunal cannot indicate the name of the accuser to either the accused or his patron unless the accuser has expressly consented. §2. This same Tribunal must consider the particular importance of the question concerning the credibility of the accuser. §3. Nevertheless, it must always be observed that any danger of violating the sacramental seal is altogether avoided.

[3] Art. 8 SST - §2. This Supreme Tribunal also judges other delicts of which a defendant is accused by the Promotor of Justice, by reason of connection of person and complicity.

aggravating factors, as provided for by law. It could also prove helpful to collect at this time testimonials of credibility with regard to the complainants and the alleged victims. An Appendix to the present *Vademecum* contains a schematic outline of useful data that those carrying out the preliminary investigation will want to compile and have at hand (cf. no. 69).

35. If, in the course of the preliminary investigation, other *notitiae de delicto* become known, these must also be looked into as part of the same investigation.

36. As mentioned above, the acquisition of the results of civil investigations (or of an entire trial before a tribunal of the state) could make the preliminary canonical investigation unnecessary. Due care must be taken, however, by those who must carry out the preliminary investigation to examine the civil investigation, since the criteria used in the latter (with regard, for example, to terms of prescription, the typology of the crime, the age of the victim, etc.) can vary significantly with respect to the norms of canon law. In these situations too, it can be advisable, in case of doubt, to consult with the CDF.

37. The preliminary investigation could also prove unnecessary in the case of a notorious and indisputable crime (given, for example, the acquisition of the civil proceedings or an admission on the part of the cleric).

b/ What juridical acts must be carried out to initiate the preliminary investigation?

38. If the competent Ordinary or Hierarch considers it appropriate to enlist another suitable person to carry out the investigation (cf. no. 21), he is to select him or her using the criteria indicated by canons 1428 §§1-2 CIC or 1093 CCEO.[4]

39. In appointing the person who carries out the investigation, and taking into account the cooperation that can be offered by lay persons in accordance with canons 228 CIC and 408 CCEO (cf. art. 13 VELM), the Ordinary or Hierarch should keep in mind that, according to canons 1717 §3 CIC and 1468 §3 CCEO, if a penal judicial process is then initiated, that same person cannot act as a judge

---

[4] C. 1428 CIC – §1. The judge or the president of a collegiate tribunal can designate an auditor, selected either from the judges of the tribunal or from persons the bishop approves for this function, to instruct the case. §2. The bishop can approve for the function of auditor clerics or lay persons outstanding for their good character, prudence and doctrine. C. 1093 CCEO – §1. A judge or the president of a collegiate tribunal can designate an auditor to instruct the case. The auditor is selected either from among the judges of the tribunal or from among the Christian faithful admitted to this office by the eparchial bishop. §2. The eparchial bishop can approve for the office of auditor members of the Christian faithful outstanding for their good character, prudence and doctrine.

in the matter. Sound practice suggests that the same criterion be used in appointing the Delegate and the Assessors in the case of an extrajudicial process.

40. In accordance with canons 1719 CIC and 1470 CCEO, the Ordinary or Hierarch is to issue a decree opening the preliminary investigation, in which he names the person conducting the investigation and indicates in the text that he or she enjoys the powers referred to in canon 1717 §3 CIC or 1468 §3 CCEO.

41. Although not expressly provided for by law, it is advisable that a priest notary be appointed (cf. c. 483 §2 CIC and c. 253 §2 CCEO, where other criteria are indicated for the choice), who assists the person conducting the preliminary investigation, for the purpose of ensuring the authenticity of the acts which have been drawn up (cf. c. 1437 §2 CIC and c. 1101 §2 CCEO).

42. It should be noted, however, that since these are not the acts of a process, the presence of the notary is not necessary for their validity.

43. In the investigative phase the appointment of a promoter of justice is not foreseen.

c/ What complementary acts can or must be carried out during the preliminary investigation?

44. Canons 1717 §2 CIC and 1468 §2 CCEO, and articles 4 §2 and 5 §2 VELM speak of protecting the good name of the persons involved (the accused, alleged victims, witnesses), so that the report will not lead to prejudice, retaliation or discrimination in their regard. The one who carries out the preliminary investigation must therefore be particularly careful to take every possible precaution to this end, since the right to a good name is one of the rights of the faithful upheld by canons 220 CIC and 23 CCEO. It should be noted, however, that those canons protect that right from illegitimate violations. Hence, should the common good be endangered, the release of information about the existence of an accusation does not necessarily constitute a violation of one's good name. Furthermore, the persons involved are to be informed that in the event of a judicial seizure or a subpoena of the acts of the investigation on the part of civil authorities, it will no longer be possible for the Church to guarantee the confidentiality of the depositions and documentation acquired from the canonical investigation.

45. In any event, especially in cases where public statements must be made, great caution should be exercised in providing information about the facts. Statements should be brief and concise, avoiding clamorous announcements, refraining completely from any premature judgment about the guilt or innocence of the person accused (since this is to be established only by an eventual penal process

aimed at verifying the basis of the accusation), and respecting any desire for privacy expressed by the alleged victims.

46. Since, as stated above, in this phase the possible guilt of the accused person has yet to be established, all care should be taken to avoid – in public statements or private communication – any affirmation made in the name of the Church, the Institute or Society, or on one's own behalf, that could constitute an anticipation of judgement on the merits of the facts.

47. It should also be noted that accusations, processes and decisions relative to delicts mentioned in art. 6 SST are subject to the secret of office. This does not prevent persons reporting – especially if they also intend to inform the civil authorities – from making public their actions. Furthermore, since not all forms of *notitiae de delicto* are formal accusations, it is possible to evaluate whether or not one is bound by the secret, always keeping in mind the respect for the good name of others referred to in no. 44.

48. Here too, consideration should be given to whether the Ordinary or Hierarch is obliged to inform the civil authorities of the reception of the *notitia de delicto* and the opening of the preliminary investigation. Two principles apply: a/ respect for the laws of the state (cf. art. 19 VELM); and b/ respect for the desire of the alleged victim, provided that this is not contrary to civil legislation. Alleged victims should be encouraged – as will be stated below (no. 56) – to exercise their duties and rights vis-à-vis the state authorities, taking care to document that this encouragement took place and to avoid any form of dissuasion with regard to the alleged victim. Relevant agreements (concordats, accords, protocols of understanding) entered into by the Apostolic See with national governments must always and in any event be observed.

49. When the laws of the state require the Ordinary or Hierarch to report a *notitia de delicto*, he must do so, even if it is expected that on the basis of state laws no action will be taken (for example, in cases where the statute of limitations has expired or the definition of the crime may vary).

50. Whenever civil judicial authorities issue a legitimate executive order requiring the surrender of documents regarding cases, or order the judicial seizure of such documents, the Ordinary or Hierarch must cooperate with the civil authorities. If the legitimacy of such a request or seizure is in doubt, the Ordinary or Hierarch can consult legal experts about available means of recourse. In any case, it is advisable to inform the Papal Representative immediately.

51. In cases where it proves necessary to hear minors or persons equivalent to them, the civil norms of the country should be followed, as well as methods suited

77

to their age or condition, permitting, for example, that the minor be accompanied by a trusted adult and avoiding any direct contact with the person accused.

52. During the investigative process, a particularly sensitive task falling to the Ordinary of Hierarch is to decide if and when to inform the person being accused.

53. In this regard, there is no uniform criterion or explicit provision in law. An assessment must be made of all the goods at stake: in addition to the protection of the good name of the persons involved, consideration must also be given, for example, to the risk of compromising the preliminary investigation or giving scandal to the faithful, and the advantage of collecting beforehand all evidence that could prove useful or necessary.

54. Should a decision be made to question the accused person, since this is a preliminary phase prior to a possible process, it is not obligatory to name an official advocate for him. If he considers it helpful, however, he can be assisted by a patron of his choice. An oath cannot be imposed on the accused person (cf. *ex analogia*, cc. 1728 §2 CIC and 1471 §2 CCEO).

55. The ecclesiastical authorities must ensure that the alleged victim and his or her family are treated with dignity and respect, and must offer them welcome, attentive hearing and support, also through specific services, as well as spiritual, medical and psychological help, as required by the specific case (cf. art. 5 VELM). The same can be done with regard to the accused. One should, however, avoid giving the impression of wishing to anticipate the results of the process.

56. It is absolutely necessary to avoid in this phase any act that could be interpreted by the alleged victim as an obstacle to the exercise of his or her civil rights vis-à-vis the civil authorities.

57. Where there exist state or ecclesiastical structures of information and support for alleged victims, or of consultation for ecclesial authorities, it is helpful also to refer to them. The purpose of these structures is purely that of advice, guidance and assistance; their analyses do not in any way constitute canonical procedural decisions.

58. To defend the good name of the persons involved and to protect the public good, as well as to avoid other factors (for example, the rise of scandal, the risk of concealment of future evidence, the presence of threats or other conduct meant to dissuade the alleged victim from exercising his or her rights, the protection of other possible victims), in accordance with art. 19 SST, the Ordinary or Hierarch

has the right, from the outset of the preliminary investigation, to impose the precautionary measures listed in canons 1722 CIC and 1473 CCEO.[5]

59. The precautionary measures found in these canons constitute a taxative list, in other words, only one or more of those delineated can be chosen.

60. This does not prevent the Ordinary or Hierarch from imposing other disciplinary measures within his power, yet these cannot be strictly defined as "precautionary measures".

d/ How are precautionary measures imposed?

61. First, it should be stated that a precautionary measure is not a penalty (since penalties are imposed only at the end of a penal process), but an administrative act whose purposes are described by the aforementioned canons 1722 CIC and 1473 CCEO. It should be clearly explained to the party in question that the measure is not penal in nature, lest he think that he has already been convicted and punished from the start. It must also be emphasized that precautionary measures must be revoked if the reason for them ceases and that they themselves cease with the conclusion of the eventual penal process. Furthermore, they can be modified (made more or less severe), if circumstances so demand. Still, particular prudence and discernment is urged in judging whether the reason that suggested them has ceased; nor is it excluded that – once revoked – they can be re-imposed.

62. It has been noted that the older terminology of *suspensio a divinis* is still frequently being used to refer to the prohibition of the exercise of ministry imposed on a cleric as a precautionary measure. It is best to avoid this term, and that of *suspensio ad cautelam*, since in the current legislation suspension is a penalty, and cannot yet be imposed at this stage. The provision would more properly be called, for example, *prohibition* from the exercise of the ministry.

63. A decision to be avoided is that of simply transferring the accused cleric from his office, region or religious house, with the idea that distancing him from the

---

[5] C. 1722 CIC – To prevent scandals, to protect the freedom of witnesses, and to guard the course of justice, the ordinary, after having heard to promotor of justice… can exclude the accused from the sacred ministry or from some office and ecclesiastical function, can impose or forbid residence in some place or territory, or can even prohibit public participation in the Most Holy Eucharist… C. 1473 CCEO – To prevent scandals, to protect the freedom of witnesses, and to guard the course of justice, the hierarch, after having heard the promotor of justice and cited the accused, at any stage and grade of the penal trial can exclude the accused from the exercise of sacred orders, an office, a ministry, or another function, can impose or forbid residence in some place or territory, or even can prohibit public reception of the Divine Eucharist…

place of the alleged crime or alleged victims constitutes a sufficient solution of the case.

64. The precautionary measures referred to in no. 58 are imposed by a singular precept, legitimately made known (cf. cc. 49ff. and 1319 CIC and 1406 and 1510ff. CCEO).

65. It should be noted that whenever a decision is made to modify or revoke precautionary measures, this must be done by a corresponding decree, legitimately made known. This will not be necessary, however, at the conclusion of the possible process, since at that moment those measures cease to have legal effect.

e/ What must be done to conclude the preliminary investigation?

66. It is recommended, for the sake of equity and a reasonable exercise of justice, that the duration of the preliminary investigation correspond to the purpose of the investigation, which is to assess the plausibility of the *notitia de delicto* and hence the existence of the *fumus delicti*. An unjustified delay in the preliminary investigation may constitute an act of negligence on the part of ecclesiastical authority.

67. If the investigation has been carried out by a suitable person appointed by the Ordinary or Hierarch, he or she is to consign all the acts of the investigation, together with a personal evaluation of its results.

68. In accordance with canons 1719 CIC and 1470 CCEO, the Ordinary or Hierarch must decree the conclusion of the preliminary investigation.

69. In accordance with art. 16 SST, once the preliminary investigation has concluded, whatever its outcome, the Ordinary or Hierarch is obliged to send, without delay, an authentic copy of the relative acts to the CDF. Together with the copy of the acts and the duly completed form found at the end of this handbook, he is to provide his own evaluation of the results of the investigation (*votum*) and to offer any suggestions he may have on how to proceed (if, for example, he considers it appropriate to initiate a penal procedure and of what kind; if he considers sufficient the penalty imposed by the civil authorities; if the application of administrative measures by the Ordinary or Hierarch is preferable; if the prescription of the delict should be declared or its derogation granted).

70. In cases where the Ordinary or Hierarch who carried out the preliminary investigation is a major Superior, it is best that he likewise transmit a copy of all documentation related to the investigation to the supreme Moderator (or to the relative Bishop in the case of Institutes or Societies of diocesan right), since they

are the persons with whom the CDF will ordinarily communicate thereafter. For his part, the supreme Moderator will send to the CDF his own *votum*, as above in no. 69.

71. Whenever the Ordinary who carried out the preliminary investigation is not the Ordinary of the place where the alleged delict was committed, he is to communicate to the latter the results of the investigation.

72. The acts are to be sent in a single copy; it is helpful if they are authenticated by a notary who is a member of the curia, unless a specific notary had been appointed for the preliminary investigation.

73. Canons 1719 CIC and 1470 CCEO state that the original of all the acts is to be kept in the secret archive of the curia.

74. Again, according to art. 16 SST, once the acts of the preliminary investigation have been sent to the CDF, the Ordinary or Hierarch is to await communications or instructions in this regard from the CDF.

75. Clearly, if other elements related to the preliminary investigation or new accusations should emerge in the meantime, these are to be forwarded to the CDF as quickly as possible, in order to be added to what is already in its possession. If it appears useful to reopen the preliminary investigation on the basis of those elements, the CDF is to be informed immediately.

IV. What can the CDF do at this point?

76. Upon receipt of the acts of the preliminary investigation, ordinarily the CDF immediately sends an acknowledgment to the Ordinary, Hierarch, Supreme Moderator (in the case of religious, also to the Congregation for Institutes of Consecrated Life and for Societies of Apostolic Life; if the cleric is from an Eastern Church, to the Congregation for Oriental Churches; and to the Congregation for the Evangelization of Peoples if the cleric belongs to a territory subject to that Dicastery), communicating – unless it had previously done so – the protocol number corresponding to the case. Reference must be made to this number in all further communication with the CDF.

77. After attentively examining the acts, the CDF can then choose to act in a variety of ways: it can archive the case; request a more thorough preliminary investigation; impose non-penal disciplinary measures, ordinarily by a penal precept; impose penal remedies or penances, or warnings or rebukes; initiate a penal process; or identify other means of pastoral response. The decision, once made, is then communicated to the Ordinary with suitable instructions for its execution.

a/ What are non-penal disciplinary measures?

78. Non-penal disciplinary measures are singular administrative acts (that is, acts of the Ordinary or Hierarch, or of the CDF) by which the accused is ordered to do or to refrain from doing something. In these cases, limits are ordinarily imposed on the exercise of the ministry, of greater or lesser extent in view of the case, and also at times the obligation of residing in a certain place. It must be emphasized that these are not penalties, but acts of governance meant to ensure and protect the common good and ecclesial discipline, and to avoid scandal on the part of the faithful.

b/ What is a penal precept?

79. The ordinary form with which these measures are imposed is the penal precept mentioned in canon 1319 §1 CIC and 1406 §1 CCEO. Canon 1406 §2 CCEO states that a warning containing the threat of penalty is equivalent to a penal precept.

80. The formalities required for a precept are those previously mentioned (cc. 49ff CIC and 1510ff CCEO). Nonetheless, since it involves a penal precept, the text must clearly indicate the penalty being threatened if the recipient of the precept were to violate the measures imposed on him.

81. It should be kept in mind that, according to canon 1319 §1 CIC, a penal precept cannot impose perpetual expiatory penalties; furthermore, the penalty must be clearly defined. Other exclusions of penalties are foreseen by canon 1406 §1 CCEO for Eastern rite faithful.

82. Such an administrative act admits recourse within the terms of law.

c/ What are penal remedies, penances and public rebukes?

83. For the definition of penal remedies, penances and public rebukes, canons 1339 and 1340 §1 CIC and canon 1427 CCEO should be consulted.[6]

---

[6] C. 1339 CIC – §1: An ordinary, personally or through another, can warn a person who is in the proximate occasion of committing a delict or upon whom after investigation, grave suspicion of having committed a delict has fallen. §2. He can also rebuke a person whose behaviour causes scandal or a grave disturbance of order, in a manner accommodated to the special conditions of the person and the deed. §3. The warning or rebuke must always be established at least by some document which is to be kept in the secret archive of the curia. C. 1340 §1 CIC: A penance, which can be imposed in the external forum, is the performance of some work of religion, piety, or charity. C. 1427 CCEO – §1: Without prejudice to particular law, a public rebuke is to occur before a notary or two witnesses or by letter, but in such a way that the reception and tenor of the letter are established by some

V. What decisions are possible in a penal process?

84. The decision that concludes the penal process, whether judicial or extrajudicial, can be of three types:

• *conviction ("constat")*, if with moral certainty the guilt of the accused is established with regard to the delict ascribed to him. In this case, the decision must indicate specifically the type of canonical sanction imposed or declared.

• *acquittal ("constat de non")*, if with moral certainty the innocence of the accused is established, inasmuch as no offence was committed, the accused did not commit the offence, the offence is not deemed a delict by the law or was committed by a person who is not imputable.

• *dismissal ("non constat")*, whenever it has not been possible to attain moral certainty with regard to the guilt of the accused, due to lack of evidence or to insufficient or conflicting evidence that the offence was in fact committed, that the accused committed the offence, or that the delict was committed by a person who is not imputable.

It is possible to provide for the public good or for the welfare of the person accused through appropriate warnings, penal remedies and other means of pastoral solicitude (cf. c. 1348 CIC).

The decision (issued by sentence or by decree) must refer to one of these three types, so that it is clear whether *"constat"*, *"constat de non"* or *"non constat"*.

VI. What penal procedures are possible?

85. By law, three penal procedures are possible: a judicial penal process; an extrajudicial penal process; or the procedure introduced by article 21 §2, 2° SST.

86. The procedure provided for in article 21 §2, 2° SST[7] is reserved for the most grave cases, concludes with a direct decision of the Supreme Pontiff and requires that, even though the commission of the delict is manifestly evident, the accused be guaranteed the right of self-defence.

---

document. §2. Care must be taken that the public rebuke itself does not result in a greater disgrace of the offender than is appropriate.

[7] Article 21 §2, 2° SST: The Congregation for the Doctrine of the Faith may: ... 2° present the most grave cases to the decision of the Roman Pontiff with regard to dismissal from the clerical state or deposition, together with dispensation from the law of celibacy, when it is manifestly evident that the delict was committed and after having given the guilty party the possibility of defending himself.

87. For the judicial penal process, the relative provisions of the law should be consulted, either in the respective Codes or in articles 8-15, 18-19, 21 §1, 22-31 SST.

88. The judicial penal process does not require a double conforming sentence; consequently, a decision rendered by a sentence in an eventual second instance becomes *res iudicata* (cf. art. 28 SST). Such a definitive sentence can be challenged only by a *restitutio in integrum*, provided elements are produced that make its injustice clear (cf. cc. 1645 CIC, 1326 CCEO), or by a complaint of nullity (cf. cc. 1619ff CIC, 1302ff CCEO). The Tribunal established for this kind of process is always collegiate and is composed of a minimum of three judges. Those who enjoy the right of appeal against a sentence of first instance include not only the accused party who considers himself unjustly aggrieved by the sentence, but also the Promoter of Justice of the CDF (cf. art. 26 §2 SST).

89. According to articles 16 and 17 SST, a judicial penal process can be carried out within the CDF or can be entrusted to a lower tribunal. With regard to the decision rendered, a specific letter of execution is sent to all interested parties.

90. Also in the course of a penal process, whether judicial or extrajudicial, the precautionary measures referred to in nos. 58-65 can be imposed on the accused.

a/ What is the extrajudicial penal process?

91. The extrajudicial penal process, sometimes called an *administrative process*, is a type of penal process that abbreviates the formalities called for in the judicial process, for the sake of expediting the course of justice without eliminating the procedural guarantees demanded by a fair trial (cf. cc. 221 CIC and 24 CCEO).

92. In the case of delicts reserved to the CDF, article 21 §2, 1° SST, derogating from canons 1720 CIC and 1486 CCEO, states that the CDF alone, in individual cases, *ex officio* or when requested by the Ordinary or Hierarch, may decide to proceed in this way.

93. Like the judicial process, the extrajudicial process can be carried out within the CDF or entrusted to a lower instance, or to the Ordinary or Hierarch of the accused, or to third parties charged with this task by the CDF, possibly at the request of the Ordinary or Hierarch. With regard to the decision rendered, a specific letter of execution is sent to all interested parties.

94. The extrajudicial penal process is carried out with slightly different formalities according to the two Codes. If questions arise concerning which Code is applicable (for example, in the case of clerics of the Latin rite who work in Eastern Churches or clerics of an Eastern rite who are active in Latin rite

circumscriptions), it will be necessary to clarify with the CDF which Code is to be followed, and then to adhere strictly to the CDF's decision.

b/ How is an extrajudicial penal process carried out according to the CIC?

95. When an Ordinary is charged by the CDF with carrying out an extrajudicial penal process, he must first decide whether to preside over the process personally or to name a delegate. He must also appoint two assessors who will assist him or his delegate in the evaluative phase. In choosing them, it would be advisable to consider the criteria set forth in canons 1424 and 1448 §1 CIC. It is also necessary to appoint a notary, according to the criteria given in no. 41. The appointment of a promoter of justice is not foreseen.

96. The aforementioned appointments are made by decree. These officials are required to take an oath to fulfil faithfully the task with which they have been entrusted and to observe secrecy. The administration of the oath must be recorded in the acts.

97. Subsequently, the Ordinary (or his delegate) must initiate the process by a decree summoning the accused. This decree must contain: the clear indication of who is being summoned; the place and time at which he must appear; the purpose for which he is being summoned, that is, to take note of the accusation (which the text of the decree is to set forth briefly) and of the corresponding proofs (which the decree need not list), and to exercise his right of self-defence.

98. Although not explicitly provided for by law in an extrajudicial process, nonetheless, since a penal matter is involved, it is most fitting that the accused, in accordance with the prescriptions of canons 1723 and 1481 §§1-2 CIC, be assisted by a procurator and/or advocate, either of his own choice or, otherwise, appointed *ex officio*. The Ordinary (or his delegate) must be informed of the appointment of the advocate by means of a suitable and authentic procuratorial mandate in accordance with canon 1484 §1 CIC, prior to the session in which the accusations and proofs are made known, in order to verify that the requirements of canon 1483 CIC have been met.[8]

99. If the accused refuses or fails to appear, the Ordinary (or his delegate) may consider whether or not to issue a second summons.

---

[8] Can. 1483 CIC – The procurator and advocate must have attained the age of majority and be of good reputation; moreover, the advocate must be a Catholic unless the diocesan bishop permits otherwise, a doctor in canon law or otherwise truly expert, and approved by the same bishop.

100. If accused refuses or fails to appear at the first or second summons, he is to be warned that the process will go forward despite his absence. This notification can be given at the time of the first summons. If the accused has failed or refused to appear, this should be noted in the acts and the process is to continue *ad ulteriora*.

101. On the day and time of the session in which the accusations and proofs are made known, the file containing the acts of the preliminary investigation is shown to the accused and to his advocate, if the latter is present. The obligation to respect the secret of office should be made known.

102. Particular attention should be given to the fact that, if the case involves the sacrament of Penance, respect must be shown for article 24 SST, which states that the name of the alleged victim is not to be revealed to the accused unless the accuser has expressly consented otherwise.

103. It is not obligatory that the assessors take part in the notification session.

104. Notification of the accusations and proofs takes place in order to give the accused the possibility of self-defence (cf. c. 1720, 1° CIC).

105. "Accusation" refers to the delict that the alleged victim or other person claims to have occurred, as this has emerged from the preliminary investigation. Setting forth the accusation means informing the accused of the delict attributed to him and any attendant details (for example, the place where it occurred, the number and eventual names of the alleged victims, the circumstances).

106. "Proofs" are all those materials collected during the preliminary investigation and any other materials acquired: first, the record of the accusations made by the alleged victims; then pertinent documents (e.g., medical records; correspondence, even by electronic means; photographs; proofs of purchase; bank records); statements made by eventual witnesses; and finally any expert opinions (medical, including psychiatric; psychological; graphological) that the person who conducted the investigation may have deemed appropriate to accept or have carried out. Any rules of confidentiality imposed by civil law should be observed.

107. All the above are referred to as "proofs" because, despite having been collected in the phase prior to the process, from the moment the extrajudicial process is opened, they automatically become a body of evidence.

108. At any stage of the process, it is legitimate for the Ordinary or his delegate to ask for the collection of further proofs, should it be considered appropriate on the basis of the results of the preliminary investigation. This can also occur at the request of the accused during the defence phase. The results will naturally be

presented to the accused during that phase. The accused is to be presented with what was collected at the defence's request, and a new session for presenting accusations and proofs is to be held, should new elements of accusation or proofs have emerged; otherwise, the material collected can be considered simply as further evidence for the defence.

109. The argument for the defence can be presented in two ways: a/ it can be accepted in session with a specific statement signed by all present (in particular by: the Ordinary or his delegate; the accused and his advocate, if any; the notary); or b/ through the setting of a reasonable time limit within which the defence can be presented in writing to the Ordinary or his delegate.

110. It should be carefully noted that, according to canon 1728 §2 CIC, the accused is not bound to confess (admit) the delict, nor can he be required to take an oath to tell the truth.

111. The argument for the defence can clearly make use of all legitimate means, as for example the request to hear its own witnesses or to present documents and expert opinions.

112. For the admission of these proofs (and, in particular, the gathering of statements of eventual witnesses), the discretionary criteria permitted to the judge by universal law on contentious trials are applicable.[9]

113. Whenever the concrete case requires it, the Ordinary or his delegate is to assess the credibility of those taking part in the process.[10] According to article 24 §2 SST, however, he is obliged to do so with regard to the credibility of the accuser should the sacrament of Penance be involved.

114. Since this is a penal process, the accuser is not obliged to take part in the process. The accuser has in fact exercised his right by contributing to the formation of the accusation and the gathering of proofs. From that moment, the accusation is carried forward by the Ordinary or his delegate.

---

[9] By analogy with canon 1527 CIC – §1. Proofs of any kind which seem useful for adjudicating the case and are licit can be brought forward.

[10] By analogy with canon 1572 CIC – In evaluating testimony, the judge, after having requested testimonial letters if necessary, is to consider the following: 1) what the condition or reputation of the person is; 2) whether the testimony derives from personal knowledge, especially from what has been seen or heard personally, or whether from opinion, rumor, or hearsay; 3) whether the witness is reliable and firmly consistent or inconsistent, uncertain, or vacillating; 4) whether the witness has co-witnesses to the testimony or is supported or not by other elements of proof.

c/ How is an extrajudicial penal process concluded according to the CIC?

115. The Ordinary or his delegate invites the two assessors to provide, within a certain reasonable time limit, their evaluation of the proofs and the arguments of the defence, in accordance with canon 1720, 2° CIC. In the decree, he can also invite them to a joint session to carry out this evaluation. The purpose of this session is evidently to facilitate analysis, discussion and debate. For such a session, which is optional but recommended, no particular juridical formalities are foreseen.

116. The entire file of the process is provided beforehand to the assessors, granting them a suitable time for study and personal evaluation. It is helpful to remind them of their obligation to observe the secret of office.

117. Although not required by law, it is helpful if the opinion of the assessors is set down in writing so as to facilitate the drafting of the subsequent final decree by the person charged to do so.

118. Similarly, if the evaluation of proofs and defence arguments takes place during a joint session, it is advisable that a series of notes on the interventions and the discussion be taken, also in the form of minutes signed by the participants. These written notes fall under the secret of office and are not to be made public.

119. Should the delict be established with certainty, the Ordinary or his delegate (cf. c. 1720, 3° CIC) must issue a decree concluding the process and imposing the penalty, penal remedy or penance that he considers most suitable for the reparation of scandal, the reestablishment of justice and the amendment of the guilty party.

120. The Ordinary should always keep in mind that, if he intends to impose a perpetual expiatory penalty, according to article 21 §2, 1° SST he must have a prior mandate from the CDF. This is a derogation, limited to these cases, from the prohibition of inflicting a perpetual penalty by decree, laid down in canon 1342 §2 CIC.

121. The list of perpetual penalties is solely that found in canon 1336 §1 CIC,[11] along with the caveats contained in canons 1337 and 1338 CIC.[12]

122. Since it involves an extrajudicial process, it should be remembered that a penal decree is not a sentence, which is issued only at the conclusion of a judicial process, even if – like a sentence – it imposes a penalty.

123. The decree in question is a personal act of the Ordinary or of his delegate, and therefore should not be signed by the assessors, but is to be authenticated by the notary.

124. In addition to the general formalities applicable in the case of every decree (cf. cc. 48-56 CIC), the penal decree must cite in summary fashion the principal elements of the accusation and the development of the process, but above all it must set forth at least briefly the reasons for the decision, both in law (listing, that is, the canons on which the decision was based – for example, those that define the delict, those that define possible mitigating, exempting or aggravating circumstances – and, however concisely, the juridical logic that led to the decision to apply them) and in fact.

125. The statement of reasons in fact is clearly the more difficult, since the author of the decree must set forth the reasons which, by comparing the matter of the accusation and the statements of the defence (which he must summarize in his

---

[11] C. 1336 CIC – §1. In addition to other penalties which the law may have established, the following are expiatory penalties which can affect an offender either perpetually, for a prescribed time, or for an indeterminate time: 1) a prohibition or an order concerning residence in a certain place or territory; 2) privation of a power, office, function, right, privilege, faculty, favor, title, or insignia, even merely honorary; 3) a prohibition against exercising those things listed under n. 2, or a prohibition against exercising them in a certain place or outside a certain place; these prohibitions are never under pain of nullity; 4) a penal transfer to another office; 5) dismissal from the clerical state.

[12] C. 1337 CIC – §1. A prohibition against residing in a certain place or territory can affect both clerics and religious; however, the order to reside in a certain place or territory can affect secular clerics and, within the limits of the constitutions, religious. §2. To impose an order to reside in a certain place or territory requires the consent of the ordinary of that place unless it is a question of a house designated for clerics doing penance or being rehabilitated even from outside the diocese.
C. 1338 CIC – §1. The privations and prohibitions listed in can. 1336, §1, nn. 2 and 3, never affect powers, offices, functions, rights, privileges, favors, titles, or insignia which are not subject to the power of the superior who establishes the penalty. §2. Privation of the power of orders is not possible but only a prohibition against exercising it or some of its acts; likewise, privation of academic degrees is not possible. §3. The norm given in can. 1335 for censures must be observed for the prohibitions listed in can. 1336, §1, n. 3.

exposition), led him to certainty concerning the commission or non-commission of the delict, or the absence of sufficient moral certainty.

126. Since not everyone possesses a detailed knowledge of canon law and its formal language, a penal decree should primarily be concerned with explaining the reasoning behind the decision, rather than being concerned about precise and detailed terminology. Where appropriate, competent persons may be called upon for assistance in this regard.

127. The notification of the entire decree (therefore not simply the dispositive part) is to take place by the legitimate means prescribed (cf. cc. 54-56 CIC[13]) and in proper form.

128. In all cases, an authenticated copy of the acts of the process (unless these had been previously forwarded) and of the notification of the decree must be sent to the CDF.

129. If the CDF decides to call to itself the extrajudicial penal process, all the formalities called for in nos. 91ff. will clearly be its responsibility, without prejudice to its right to request, if necessary, the cooperation of lower instances.

d/ How is an extrajudicial penal process carried out according to the CCEO?

130. As was stated in no. 94, the extrajudicial penal process as described in the CCEO is carried out with certain distinctive characteristics proper to that law. For the purpose of greater ease of explanation and to avoid repetitions, only those distinctive characteristics will be indicated: consequently, the following adjustments must be introduced to the praxis outlined above and shared with the CIC.

131. Above all, it must be remembered that the prescription of canon 1486 CCEO must be strictly followed, under pain of invalidity of the penal decree.

---

[13] C. 54 CIC – §1. A singular decree whose application is entrusted to an executor takes effect from the moment of execution; otherwise, from the moment it is made known to the person by the authority of the one who issued it. §2. To be enforced, a singular decree must be made known by a legitimate document according to the norm of law. C. 55 CIC – Without prejudice to the prescripts of canons 37 and 51, when a very grave reason prevents the handing over of the written text of a decree, the decree is considered to have been made known if it is read to the person to whom it is destined in the presence of a notary or two witnesses. After a written record of what has occurred has been prepared, all those present must sign it. C. 56 CIC – A decree is considered to have been made known if the one for whom it is destined has been properly summoned to receive or hear the decree but, without a just cause, did not appear or refused to sign.

132. In the extrajudicial penal process according to the CCEO, there is no mention of assessors, but the presence of the promoter of justice is obligatory.

133. The session for the notification of the accusation and proofs must take place with the obligatory presence of the promoter of justice and the notary.

134. According to canon 1486 §1, 2° CCEO, the session of notification and consequently the presentation of the defence is to take place solely with oral arguments. Nevertheless, this does not exclude, for such arguments, the defence being presented in written form.

135. Particular attention should be given to the question whether, on the basis of the gravity of the delict, the penalties listed in canon 1426 §1 CCEO are indeed adequate for achieving the provisions of canon 1401 CCEO. In deciding the penalty to be imposed, canons 1429[14] and 1430[15] CCEO should be observed.

136. The Hierarch or his delegate should always remember that, according to article 21 §2, 1° SST, the prohibitions of canon 1402 §2 CCEO are abrogated. Therefore he is able to impose a perpetual expiatory penalty by decree, having obtained the prior mandate of the CDF required by the same article 21 §2, 1° SST.

137. For the drawing up of the penal decree, the same criteria indicated in nos. 119-126 apply.

138. Notification of the decree will then take place in the terms of canon 1520 CCEO and in proper form.

---

[14] C. 1429 CCEO – §1. The prohibition against living in a certain place or territory can affect only clerics and religious or members of a society of common life in the manner of religious; an injunction to live in a certain place or territory affects only clerics enrolled in an eparchy, without prejudice to institutes of consecrated life. §2. For the imposition of the injunction to live in a certain place or territory, the consent of the hierarch of that place is required, unless it is a case either of a house of an institute of consecrated life of papal or patriarchal right, in which case the consent of the competent superior is required, or of a house designated for the correction and reformation of clerics of several eparchies.

[15] C. 1430 CCEO – §1. Penal deprivations can affect only those powers, offices, ministries, functions, rights, privileges, faculties, benefits, titles, insignia, which are subject to the power of the authority that establishes the penalty, or of the hierarch who initiated the penal trial or imposed it by decree; the same applies to penal transfer to another office. §2. Deprivation of the power of sacred orders is not possible, but only a prohibition against exercising all or some acts of orders, in accordance with common law; nor is deprivation of academic degrees possible.

139. For those things not mentioned here, reference should be made to what has been stated regarding the extrajudicial process according to the CIC, including the possibility that the process will take place in the CDF.

e/ Does the penal decree fall under the secret of office?

140. As previously mentioned (cf. no. 47), the procedural acts and the decision fall under the secret of office. All taking part in the process, in any capacity, should be constantly reminded of this.

141. The decree is to be made known in its entirety to the accused. The notification must be made to his procurator, if he has one.

VII. What can happen once a penal procedure ends?

142. According to the type of procedure employed, there are different possibilities available for those who were parties in the process.

143. If it was the procedure mentioned in article 21 §2, 2° SST, inasmuch as it concerns an act of the Roman Pontiff, no appeal or recourse is admitted (cf. cc. 333 §3 CIC and 45 §3 CCEO).

144. If it was a penal judicial process, the possibility of a legal challenge exists, namely, a complaint of nullity, *restitutio in integrum*, or appeal.

145. According to article 20, 1° SST, the only tribunal of second instance for appeals is that of the CDF.

146. To present an appeal, the prescriptions of law are to be followed, noting carefully that article 28, 2° SST modified the time limits for the presentation of an appeal, imposing a peremptory time limit of one month, to be calculated according to what is laid down in canons 202 §1 CIC and 1545 §1 CCEO.

147. If it was an extrajudicial penal process, recourse can be made against the decree that concluded it, within the terms provided by law, namely, by canons 1734ff. CIC and 1487 CCEO (cf. Section VIII).

148. According to canons 1353 CIC and 1319 and 1487 §2 CCEO, appeals and recourses have a suspensive effect on the penalty.

149. Since the penalty is suspended and things return to a phase analogous to that prior to the process, precautionary measures remain in force with the same caveats and procedures mentioned in nos. 58-65.

VIII. What should be done in case of recourse against a penal decree?

150. The law provides different procedures, according to the two Codes.

a/ What does the CIC provide for in case of recourse against a penal decree?

151. According to canon 1734 CIC, whoever intends to present a recourse against a penal decree must first seek its revocation or emendation from the author (the Ordinary or his delegate) within the peremptory time limit of ten useful days from the legitimate notification of the decree.

152. According to canon 1735, the author, within thirty days after receiving the petition, can respond by emending his own decree (but before proceeding in this case, it is best to consult the CDF immediately), or by rejecting the petition. He also has the faculty of not responding at all.

153. Against an emended decree, the rejection of the petition, or the silence of its author, the one making recourse can apply to the CDF directly or through the author of the decree (cf. c. 1737 §1 CIC) or through a procurator, within the peremptory time limit of fifteen useful days provided for by canon 1737 §2 CIC.[16]

154. If hierarchical recourse is presented to the author of the decree, he must immediately transmit it to the CDF (cf. c. 1737 §1 CIC). Thereafter (and also in the case that the recourse was presented directly to the CDF), the author of the decree need only await possible instructions or requests from the CDF, which in any case will inform him about the result of the examination of the recourse.

b/ What does the CCEO provide for in case of recourse against a penal decree?

155. The CCEO provides a simpler procedure than that of the CIC. In fact, canon 1487 §1 CCEO provides only that recourse be sent to the CDF within ten useful days from the decree's notification.

156. The author of the decree in this case need only await instructions or requests from the CDF, which in any case will inform him about the result of the examination of the recourse. However, if the author is the Ordinary, he must take note of the suspensive effects of the appeal, mentioned in no. 148 above.

IX. Is there anything that should always be kept in mind?

157. From the time of the *notitia de delicto*, the accused has the right to present a petition to be dispensed from all the obligations connected with the clerical state, including celibacy, and, concurrently, from any religious vows. The Ordinary or Hierarch must clearly inform him of this right. Should the cleric decide to make use of this possibility, he must write a suitable petition, addressed to the Holy Father, introducing himself and briefly indicating the reasons for which he is

---

[16] C. 1737 §2 CIC – Recourse must be proposed within the peremptory time limit of fifteen useful days, which... run according to the norm of can. 1735.

seeking the dispensation. The petition must be clearly dated and signed by the petitioner. It is to be transmitted to the CDF, together with the *votum* of the Ordinary or Hierarch. In turn, the CDF will forward it and – if the Holy Father accepts the petition – will transmit the rescript of dispensation to the Ordinary or Hierarch, asking him to provide for legitimate notification to the petitioner.

158. For all singular administrative acts decreed or approved by the CDF, the possibility of recourse is provided by article 27 SST.[17] To be admitted, the recourse must clearly specify what is being sought (*petitum*) and contain the reasons in law (*in iure*) and in fact (*in facto*) on which it is based. The one making recourse must always make use of an advocate, provided with a specific mandate.

159. If an Episcopal Conference, in response to the request made by the CDF in 2011, has already provided its own written guidelines for dealing with cases of the sexual abuse of minors, this text should also be taken into account.

160. It sometimes happens that the *notitia de delicto* concerns a cleric who is already deceased. In this case, no type of penal procedure can be initiated.

161. If a reported cleric dies during the preliminary investigation, it will not be possible to open a subsequent penal procedure. In any case, it is recommended that the Ordinary or Hierarch inform the CDF all the same.

162. If an accused cleric dies during the penal process, this fact should be communicated to the CDF.

163. If, in the phase of the preliminary investigation, an accused cleric has lost his canonical status as a result of a dispensation or a penalty imposed in another proceeding, the Ordinary or Hierarch should assess whether it is suitable to carry on the preliminary investigation, for the sake of pastoral charity and the demands of justice with regard to the alleged victims. If the loss of canonical status occurs once a penal process has already begun, the process can in any case be brought to its conclusion, if for no other reason than to determine responsibility in the possible delict and to impose potential penalties. In fact, it should be remembered that, in the determination of a more serious delict (*delictum gravius*), what matters

---

[17] Article 27 SST – Recourse may be had against singular administrative acts which have been decreed or approved by the Congregation for the Doctrine of the Faith in cases of reserved delicts. Such recourse must be presented within the preemptory period of sixty canonical days to the Ordinary Session of the Congregation (the *Feria* IV) which will judge on the merits of the case and the lawfulness of the Decree. Any further recourse as mentioned in art. 123 of the Apostolic Constitution *Pastor Bonus* is excluded.

is that the accused was a cleric at the time of the alleged delict, not at the time of the proceeding.

164. Taking into account the 6 December 2019 Instruction on the confidentiality of legal proceedings, the competent ecclesiastical authority (Ordinary or Hierarch) should inform the alleged victim and the accused, should they request it, in suitable ways about the individual phases of the proceeding, taking care not to reveal information covered by the pontifical secret or the secret of office, the divulging of which could cause harm to third parties.

***

This *Vademecum* does not claim to replace the training of practitioners of canon law, especially with regard to penal and procedural matters. Only a profound knowledge of the law and its aims can render due service to truth and justice, which are especially to be sought in matters of *graviora delicta* by reason of the deep wounds they inflict upon ecclesial communion.

The accompanying Tabella/Tabular Summary is included on the next pages.

TABULAR SUMMARY FOR CASES OF *DELICTA RESERVATA*

DIOCESE/INSTITUTE OF INCARDINATION	
CHURCH *SUI IURIS* (if Eastern)	
ORDINARY	
CDF PROT. N° (if known)	
CLERIC'S FULL SURNAME(S)	
CLERIC'S FULL FIRST NAME(S)	
OFFICIAL I.D. (photocopy if available)	

SIGNIFICANT DATES OF THE CLERIC

Date of Birth		Diaconal Ordination		Age	
Perpetual Vows		Priestly Ordination		Years in Ministry	

POSSIBLE PREVIOUS PLACES OF INCARDINATION	
MINISTRY OUTSIDE OF DIOCESE/INSTITUTE OF INCARDINATION	
CLERIC'S CURRENT ADDRESS	
ADVOCATE/PROCURATOR (signed copy of mandate)	
ADVOCATE/PROCURATOR'S ADDRESS	

MINISTRY

Year(s)	Parish/Organization	Place	Appointment/Responsibility

ACCUSATION(S) OF *DELICTA RESERVATA* AGAINST THE CLERIC

Date of alleged delict(s)	Name and surname of alleged victim	Date of Birth	Place, frequency, and details of alleged delict(s)	Identity of person bringing allegation(s) & date of denunciation to ecclesiastical authority

OTHER PROBLEMATIC BEHAVIOUR/OTHER ACCUSATIONS

Year(s)	Description

CIVIL PROCEEDINGS AGAINST THE CLERIC		
Year	Type	Outcome of civil proceedings/Sentence (photocopy if possible)

MEASURES ADOPTED BY ECCLESIASTICAL AUTHORITY	
Year(s)	Description

CLERIC'S REMUNERATION

CLERIC'S RESPONSE TO ACCUSATION(S)	
Year	Response (Admission, denial, refusal to cooperate, etc.)

ORDINARY'S OPINION/*VOTUM*

Date

In regions where there is no surname, please indicate the name of the cleric's father.

This Tabular Summary is intended to be a guide to summarize the case and does not replace the acts of the preliminary investigation. Please include the Summary along with the acts of the investigation.

If possible, also send the Tabular Summary in Word format to: disciplinaryoffice@cfaith.va.

Version 1.0 – 16.07.2020

ADVISORY OPINIONS

INTRODUCTORY NOTE

The following opinions were assembled by the members of the Publications Advisory Board from among those submitted to the Society for publication. The opinions carry only the weight of the persons named at the end of each opinion. They do not represent the opinion of the diocese or institution to which the author is affiliated, nor that of the Canon Law Society of America. Advisory opinions are not authentic interpretations of the law but reflect the scholarly and practical insights of the contributors.

The opinions are arranged according to the canons of the *Code of Canon Law* and the *Code of Canons of the Eastern Churches*. The original questions have been abbreviated or summarized, and the opinions lightly edited to protect the anonymity of the inquirer and to conform to the style of Canon Law Society of America publications.

The Publications Advisory Board expresses gratitude to the canonists who participated in this year's publication. The continued success of this annual project is a result of their willingness to share their time and talent in service to this important work.

The Canon Law Society of America is interested in receiving opinions that members have formulated in response to specific inquiries and inquiries in need of responses. It also welcomes the participation of members who wish to be involved in this annual project by offering to render opinions to inquiries received by the Board.

Inquiries or contributions may be directed to:

Canon Law Society of America
415 Michigan Avenue NE
Suite 101
Washington, DC 20017-4502
admin@clsa.org

Canon 285, §1 and §2; CCEO Canon 382

On the Carrying of a Firearm by a Priest in Church as a Protective Measure

Father Joseph developed a passion for the outdoors as a young boy. His father taught him how to use guns for hunting and insisted that he take a gun safety course. Upon graduation from high school, Joseph entered the U. S. Marines and received extensive training in the use of weapons. After he was ordained, Father Joseph continued to hunt and, after having met the local civil requirements, began to carry a firearm because of the violence that occasionally erupts in his area. He volunteered for the local police reserves, and when Father Joseph is needed for crowd control at fairs and parades, he carries a gun. Recently, he was asked by the parish pastoral council whether, in the event that one of the parishioners who carries a firearm for protection to Mass was unavailable, he would stand, with his firearm concealed, in the rear of the church when not celebrating Mass to prevent someone from doing violence in the church.

Opinion

If this scenario had arisen before the 1983 Code of Canon Law was promulgated, this scenario would be much easier to analyze. Canon 138 of the 1917 code specified various things that clerics must avoid. "Clerics shall entirely abstain from all those things that are indecent to their state; . . . they shall not carry arms, except when there is just cause for fearing." The analysis likely would have come down to whether there was a sufficient level of fear to warrant the priest carrying a gun and, possibly, whether the priest was the only one able to be a substitute for the parishioners who usually handled the role.

Noticeably absent from both the 1983 Latin code and the 1990 Eastern code is any mention of the use of firearms in any capacity. nowhere does either code repeat the specific prohibition found in the 1917 CIC that clerics may not carry arms "except when there is just cause for fearing."

In order to analyze the appropriateness of what is asked of the priest in the proposed scenario, we can start by looking in the codes for a more general statement about what is and is not acceptable or recommended behavior for a presbyter. Canon 285 §1 of the Latin code states: "Clerics are to refrain completely from all those things which are unbecoming to their state, according to the prescripts of particular law." Similarly, canon 382 of the Eastern code directs: "Clerics are to abstain completely from all those things unbecoming to their state, according to the norms determined in detail by particular law, and also to avoid those things which are alien to it." Furthermore, §2 of canon 285 of the Latin code goes on to declare: "Clerics are to avoid those things which, although not unbecoming, are nevertheless foreign to the clerical state."

Is there any support for allowing the priest to carry a gun in church as our scenario asks? Authors John Abbo and Jerome Hannan cited as justification for the carrying of arms by clerics their natural right of self-defense.[1] Arguably, for a person to carry a firearm because of local violence and to protect crowds at fairs and parades is not patently unbecoming. The 1992 *Catechism of the Catholic Church* states: "Legitimate defense can be not only a right but a grave duty for one who is responsible for the lives of others. The defense of the common good requires that an unjust aggressor be rendered unable to cause harm. For this reason, those who legitimately hold authority also have the right to use arms to repel aggressors against the civil community entrusted to their responsibility" (2265).

This begs many questions, such as whether a priest, who is ordained to be an *alter Christus*, should be engaged in defending others to this extreme. Does he "legitimately hold authority?" Is he "responsible for the lives of others?" Is the parish a "civil community entrusted to [his] authority?" Is there a difference in the priest carrying a gun at parades and fairs and him carrying a gun within his church building? Is he the pastor; if not, what does the pastor say about this proposition? Is there particular law on the topic?

A tangential issue is whether Father Joseph should refrain from serving in the police reserves when it would require carrying a firearm, even for the laudable purpose of maintaining public order. It is the recommendation of this canonist that he refrain from serving in the police reserves and instead volunteer as the chaplain for the police reserves without the responsibility of carrying a firearm.

As to carrying a concealed weapon in the rear of the church, it seems much better that this task be employed by a competent lay person rather than by Father Joseph. Consideration should be given to hiring a retired or off-duty law enforcement officer to help with protection. If he continues to persist in wanting to carry a gun and to fill the role described in this scenario, Father Joseph would be well-advised to submit these matters to his bishop for consideration and determination.

Msgr. Charles M. Mangan, JCL

---

[1] John A. Abbo and Jerome D. Hannan, *The Sacred Canons: A Concise Presentation of the Current Disciplinary Norms of the Church*, vol. 1 (St. Louis, B. Herder Company, 1957).

CANON 291 AND THE 1980 *NORMAE PROCEDURALES*, ART. 4

SUSPENSIO AD CAUTELAM
FOR PRIESTS REQUESTING "LAICIZATION"

When a priest petitions to be dispensed from the obligation of celibacy (c. 291), *is a diocesan bishop or major superior of a clerical institute of pontifical right still obliged to impose the* suspensio ad cautelam *(Normae, art. 4)? If so, does this suspension have the nature of a penalty?*

OPINION

Apart from the case of the "invalidity of sacred ordination" (c. 290, 1°), only the Roman Pontiff can grant "a dispensation from the obligation of celibacy" (c. 291). Further, article 4 of the 1980 *Normae procedurales* states that

> After receiving the petition [for a dispensation from the obligation of celibacy], the ordinary is to decide whether to proceed further, and, in an affirmative case, he is to suspend [*suspendat*] the petitioner from the exercise of sacred orders *ad cautelam*, unless, in order to protect the good name of the [petitioning] priest or to care for the good of the community, he judges that their exercise is truly necessary.[1]

---

[1]   Sacred Congregation for the Doctrine of the Faith, normae procedurales de modo procedendi in examine et resolutione petitionum quae dispensationem a caelibatu respiciunt *Ordinarius compotens*, 14 October 1980, art. 4, in *AAS* 72 (1980) 1136–1137. "Recepta petitione, decernat Ordinarius an sit locus procedendi, et, in casu affirmativo, oratorem ab exercitio sacrorum Ordinum ad cautelam suspendat, nisi, ad protegendam bonam famam ipsius sacerdotis vel ad bonum communitatis tuendum, huiusmodi exercitium prorsus necessarium esse iudicaverit." These procedural norms were prefaced by a circular letter: idem, circular letter to ordinaries and religious superiors on the process for examining and proceeding with a petition for a dispensation from celibacy *Per Litteras*, 14 October 1980, in *AAS* 72 (1980) 1132–1135. The substantial norms, however, were not published in the *Acta*, but were sent to ordinaries; they were subsequently published as idem, normae substantiales de dispensatione a sacerdotali coelibatu ad instantiam partis (ad usum internum Sacrae Congregationis) *Praeterquam aliis*, 14 October 1980, in *Collectanea documentorum ad causas pro dispensatione super "rato et non consummato" et a lege sacri coelibatus obtinenda inde a Codice Iuris Canoni 1917,* Congregatio de Cultu Divino et Disciplina Sacramentorum (ed.), Città del Vaticano, 2004, 157–158.

In order to answer the question of whether or not this norm is still in force, its specific juridic nature must first be determined. For the sake of simplicity, the juridic categories of the 1983 Code will be used.

Since there is no evidence of papal delegation of legislative power or of approval *in forma specifica*, it is safe to conclude that the *Normae* are *administrative* rather than *legislative*.[2] Further, since—as is clear from Lohse's magisterial 2005–2006 study[3]—the specific norm under consideration was "essentially a canonical innovation," there being no previous law upon which it depends, it is also safe to conclude that the norm properly belongs to the category of what Huels terms "independent general administrative norms."[4] To state this negatively, the norm is neither a law (*lex* of Book I, Title I), nor a general executory decree (cc. 31–33), nor an instruction (c. 34). Positively, "this category of independent general administrative norms admits of juridical innovations, that is, new binding norms not foreseen in previous legislation but always subject to the principle of legality."[5]

The question now becomes one of possible revocation. Since the norm in question is neither a law nor dependent upon a previous law, canon 6 regarding the abrogation of previous laws does not apply.[6] Although the norm is neither a general executory decree nor an instruction, nevertheless canons 33–34 concerning revocation can still be applied, *mutatis mutandis*. Hence, independent general administrative norms cease to have force by explicit or implicit revocation.[7] As is again clear from Lohse's study, the *Normae* were not expressly revoked; on the contrary, they have been explicitly confirmed numerous times. For example:

> On February 8 of [1989], the Secretary of State confirmed the competency of the Congregation for Divine Worship and the Discipline of the Sacraments [over such matters] and instructed that the

---

[2] J.M. Huels, "Independent General Administrative Norms in Documents of the Roman Curia," in *The Jurist*, 76 (2016) 93.

[3] E. Lohse, "The Origin and Nature of the Suspension *ad cautelam* of Article 4 of the 1980 *Normae procedurales* for Dispensations from Celibacy: Part I," in *Periodica de re canonica*, 94 (2005), 647–680; idem, "The Origin and Nature of the Suspension *ad cautelam* of Article 4 of the 1980 *Normae procedurales* for Dispensations from Celibacy: Part II," in *Periodica de re canonica*, 95 (2006) 69–107.

[4] J.M. Huels, "Independent General Administrative Norms," 91.

[5] Ibid., 104.

[6] Even if it were a law, since the code does not completely reorder the matter, it would remain in force (*CIC*/1983, c. 6 §1, 4°). E. Lohse, "Origin and Nature, Part II," 101.

[7] Cf. *CIC*/1983, c. 33 §2; 34 §3.

circular letter and procedural norms which had been issued by the Congregation for the Doctrine of the Faith in 1980 would now bind both Congregations simultaneously. The provision of the suspension *ad cautelam* in article 4 would remain binding.[8]

Two years later the *Normae* were again explicitly confirmed in a letter sent to the NCCB containing a list of required documents to include in the dossier. The two most salient points of the letter for this study are:

4. A *document that demonstrates that the Petitioner has been suspended from the exercise of the sacred ministry*, once the Ordinary has reviewed the "Curriculum" and decided to accept the formal request of the Petitioner for a dispensation—thereby avoiding all possible scandal and protecting his reputation.

5. A *Decree nominating the Instructor of the case and an ecclesiastical Notary*, including the explicit statement of the obligation to proceed according to the "Substantial and Procedural Norms" promulgated by the Congregation for the Doctrine of the Faith (*AAS* 14 October 1980, pp. 1132–1137).[9]

Finally, Lohse states on his own authority that "Identical copies of this same letter from the Congregation were distributed again to United States bishops during their *ad limina* visits throughout the year 2004."[10]

Having established that the norm is still in force, the specific juridic nature of the *suspensio ad cautelam* must now be determined. Lohse, having examined the question thoroughly, concludes:

---

8 E. Lohse, "Origin and Nature, Part II," 102, referencing Secretariat of State, letter confirming the validity of the 1980 *Normae* and competence of the Congregation for Divine Worship and Discipline of the Sacraments in petitions for laicization, 8 February 1989, in *Notitiae* 25 (1989) 485.

9 Congregation for Divine Worship and the Discipline of the Sacraments, letter to the NCCB regarding documents necessary for the instruction of a case for dispensation from the obligations of priestly ordination, 19 April 1991, in *Roman Replies and CLSA Advisory Opinions* (1991), Washington, DC, CLSA, 1991, 2–4. The Latin original of this list of documents, together with official translations into the principal modern languages, is found in Congregatio de cultu divino et disciplina sacramentorum, *Collectanea documentorum ad causas pro dispensatione super "rato et non consummato" et a lege sacri coelibatus obtinenda* (Città del Vaticano: Libreria editrice Vaticana, 2004), 185–198.

10 E. Lohse, "Origin and Nature, Part II," 104. For additional references, see R.J. Kaslyn, "Canon 290 and Loss of the Clerical State," in *Studia canonica*, 49 (2015), 403–409.

Although the authors do not comment on the 1980 change in phrasing from *clericus prohibendus est* [*CIC*/1917, c. 1997] to *Ordinarius oratorem suspendat* [art. 4], it seems reasonable to conclude that neither of these usages [is] used technically [in] the sense of a penalty or censure. It seems likely that [the] canonists [who drafted it] were simply not overly scrupulous in their use of these terms. Commentators had interchanged the terms "prohibition" and "suspension" for years, and the substitution of *suspendat* for *prohibendus est* does not seem to indicate any alteration of the sense of the norm. Like [*CIC*/1917] c. 1997, article 4 of the 1980 norms simply indicates that the priest (*orator*) is not to be permitted to exercise his priestly ministry. Eventually, the promulgation of the 1983 Code ... helped to clarify any confusion in this area. In a revised version of the old c. 1997, c. 1709 §2 of the new Code simply says that once the libellus has been sent, the cleric is forbidden to exercise orders: *Misso libello, clericus ordines exercere ipso iure vetatur.* All reference to a prohibition or a suspension has been dropped, no doubt in part to bring greater clarity.[11]

In short, "Despite the change in terminology from a prohibition to a suspension, article 4 still indicates that the cleric is simply forbidden to use the power of orders. The suspension does not convey any sense of a penalty or censure."[12] It is, therefore, a "suspension" in an improper, non-technical sense. A future revision of the *Normae* might consider referring to it as a *vetitum* or simple prohibition in order to convey its juridic nature more clearly and to correspond to the new verb in canon 1709 §2 ("*vetatur*").

Finally, a word regarding the *ratio normae* is in order.

Simply put, the Church continues to be wary of the possibility that something may turn up [in the instruction of the case] that could call the validity of the petitioner's ordination into question. Such a discovery is less likely in petitions for dispensations from celibacy than in cases challenging the validity of obligations, but the Church continues to err on the side of caution. The Church requires the suspension *ad cautelam*, not *ad necessitatem*. The requirement, [therefore], is no longer absolute. The legislator has extended permission to the Ordinary to use his prudent judgment in balancing the Church's concern for the validity of the sacraments with the

---

[11] E. Lohse, "Origin and Nature, Part II," 91.
[12] Ibid., 95.

protection of other basic principles which could also be at stake, e.g., the right to a good name (cf. c. 220) and the safeguarding of the common good (cf. c. 223).[13]

In the current climate of justicialism, in which a prohibition of the exercise of orders is widely perceived as being indicative of a credible accusation of sexual abuse (cf. c. 1722), the ordinary must consider very carefully indeed whether or not it is truly warranted in each case. Since the petitioner's right to a good name (c. 220) can certainly be injured by such a prohibition, it would seem that the ordinary ought to hear the petitioner before issuing the decree (c. 50). If the ordinary decides to impose the prohibition, this decree must be issued in writing and communicated to the petitioner, "with the reasons at least summarily expressed" (c. 51). Finally, if the petitioner considers himself aggrieved by this decree, he may take recourse according to canons 1732–1739. Such recourse, since it does not concern a judicial sentence or decree which imposes or declares a penalty in the strict sense, does not have a suspensive effect (cf. c. 1353).

Rev. Brian T. Austin, FSSP, JCD, PhD

---

[13] Ibid., 94.

CANON 294

ECCLESIASTICAL CIRCUMSCRIPTIONS AND THEIR RELATIONSHIP WITH THE DIOCESAN BISHOP

What is the relationship of the faithful in personal ecclesiastical circumscriptions to the local diocesan bishop?

OPINION

The Apostolic See, in the *Annual General Statistical Questionnaire*, asks diocesan bishops the number of priests in the ecclesiastical circumscription of the diocese, their country of origin and whether they are diocesan or religious. The fact that the diocesan bishop is answering these questions indicates the close relationship between himself and any personal Ecclesiastical Circumscription.

Canons 215 and 216 of the 1917 Code required that ecclesiastical circumscriptions be territorial within a diocese and an apostolic indult was needed, for example, to establish personal parishes for an ethnic group of the faithful.

After World War II, Pope Pius XII provided for the pastoral care of refugees and migrants in his apostolic constitution *Exsul Familia* in 1952. Chaplains for migrants were granted special faculties to facilitate pastoral care without receiving the power of jurisdiction or governance.

The Second Vatican Council admitted personal criteria in ecclesiastical organisation. The decree *Christus Dominus* 11 held that the essential element of a particular Church is personal, being a "portion of the people of God". Personal factors are crucial to determine the communitarian aspect of the makeup of a community.

After Vatican II, the Code of Canon Law needed revision. The Synod of Bishops in 1967 approved the principles to guide the revision of the code. The eighth principle stated: "The principle of territoriality in the exercise of ecclesiastical government is to be revised somewhat, for contemporary apostolic factors seem to recommend personal jurisdictional units. Therefore, the new code is to affirm the following principle: generally speaking the portion of the people of God to be governed are to be determined territorially; however, if it is advantageous, other factors can be admitted as criteria for determining a community of the faithful, at least along with territoriality."

Territorial prelatures are particular churches (canon 368). The Tokelau Islands near Samoa constitute a personal prelature governed by a prelate who is a monsignor. There are not enough faithful and financial resources in the Tokelau Islands to establish a diocese at present.

Personal prelatures, as outlined by *Presbyterorum Ordinis* 10, are regulated by canons 294-297. A prelature is governed by a prelate and is personal because personal characteristics determine who are members. Eduardo Baura concludes "personal prelatures are personal circumscriptions which are added to dioceses in order to attend to peculiar pastoral needs of the faithful belonging to different dioceses, governed by a prelate as its proper Ordinary, who is helped in his pastoral task by its own presbyterium". A personal prelature can erect its own seminary and can have lay people committed to the mission of the prelature. The personal Prelature of Opus Dei is truly "personal", but within Opus Dei there are divisions into regions that have territorial limits. Therefore, Opus Dei has simultaneously both personal and territorial dimensions.

The decree *Christus Dominus* 43 taught that military vicariates were to be erected because the military and armed forces (Army, Navy and Air Force) needed special pastoral care as a result of their exceptional circumstances. The apostolic constitution of Pope John Paul II, *Spirituali militum curae*, in 1986 described the power of the military ordinary as personal, ordinary, proper and cumulative with the power of diocesan bishops. The power of governance over the faithful is cumulative if the faithful simultaneously come under the governance of the ordinariate and the diocese. "Cumulative" comes from the Latin *cumulare* meaning "to accumulate."

A military ordinariate is juridically similar to a diocese and is governed by statutes from the Apostolic See. The power of the military ordinary is over Christ's faithful who may simultaneously belong to the local diocese yet still be under the jurisdiction of the military ordinary. These faithful include members of the armed forces and their families and whoever else is determined to be a member according to the statutes. The faithful have a choice to receive pastoral care from the diocese or the military ordinariate. If there is no priest at a small, local military base, the faithful can receive pastoral care from the local parish priest and diocesan bishop. All the faithful of the ordinariate are faithful of the diocese, but all the faithful of the diocese are not necessarily faithful of the ordinariate. However, if the faithful in the military ordinariate want to be married or process a declaration of the marriage nullity case, then they must approach the military ordinary.

The episcopal conference can request the Apostolic See to establish a personal diocese for an ethnic group or the indigenous people of a country (cf. c 372). The

Anglican Church in New Zealand has a bishop for the Anglican, Maori people. During the 1980's the New Zealand Catholic Bishops Conference applied to the Apostolic See to have a bishop for the Catholic Maori people. Eventually, the Apostolic See declined the application.

Ritual ordinariates are ordinariates established to care the faithful of oriental rites in countries where the oriental hierarchy does not exist. In such a situation a Latin rite pastor is given the power of governance.

Another example of a personal ecclesiastical circumscription is the Personal Apostolic Administration of Saint John Maria Vianney in the diocese of Campos in Brazil. It was established to enable a schismatic traditionalist bishop, with his priests and faithful to return to full communion in the Catholic Church in 2002. Significantly it is an apostolic administration (c. 371 § 2).

Pope Benedict XVI allowed for the establishment of personal ordinariates for the faithful coming from the Anglican Communion on 9 November 2009 with his apostolic constitution *Anglicanorum coetibus*.[1] This ordinariate aimed to facilitate groups of Anglicans coming into full communion with the Catholic Church. There had already been the so-called *Pastoral Provision* for some communities of Episcopalians in the United states. The ordinariate for former Anglicans was established by the Congregation for the Doctrine of the Faith and was made accountable to it. According to Article 8 of *Anglicanorum coetibus,* the priests of the ordinariate exercise their ministry mutually with the parish priests of the diocese. In fact, when there is no priest of the ordinariate for a parish, the parish priest of the diocese can exercise his ministry in the ordinariate parish as a supply priest. Also, the priests of the ordinariate in their pastoral ministry must collaborate with the pastoral plans of the diocese. When a former Anglican desires to be part of the ordinariate, this desire must be made in writing. Then the person must make a profession of faith and if necessary, receive the sacraments of initiation. Someone who is previously baptised as a Catholic cannot join the ordinariate unless the person is a spouse or child of a member of the ordinariate. Because the ordinariate was established to facilitate the faithful from the Anglican Communion coming into full communion with the Catholic Church, other members of Christ's faithful are excluded. The faithful of the ordinariate can freely participate in parishes of the diocese and receive all their pastoral care from priests. Priests of the ordinariate may be elected to the council of priests of the diocese. in those parishes. Although the ordinariate has its own distinct liturgy which is similar to the Latin Church, it cannot be considered a church *sui iuris*

---

[1] Benedict XVI, apostolic constitution *Anglicanorum coetibus*, November 4, 2009, AAS 101 (2009) 985-990.

similar to an oriental church. The status of an ordinariate for former Anglicans is very different to a military vicariate. A member of the ordinariate can validly marry before a priest of the diocese without any need for permission and can obtain from the local ordinary a dispensation from form or disparity of cult. Also, a member of the ordinariate may approach the tribunal in the diocese for a declaration of nullity.

Monsignor Brendan Daly

CANON 603

TRANSFER OF A DIOCESAN HERMIT OR HERMITESS

A diocesan hermit or hermitess of the Latin Church would like to relocate to another diocese and continue in the eremitic life. What is required of the hermitess and the diocesan bishop in order to effect this transfer?

OPINION

In the first place, a distinction must be made between a *public* and *private* vow. "A vow is public if a legitimate superior accepts it in the name of the Church; otherwise, it is private" (c. 1192, §1). One who has made a *private* vow to live the eremitic life still "has the right to freedom of movement,"[1] unless an additional vow of stability was also made. In this latter case, a dispensation from a private vow of stability ought to be sought from a local ordinary or pastor, either of whom is competent, even with respect to travelers (c. 1196, 1°).

One who has made a *public* profession, on the other hand, "in the hands of the diocesan bishop [of] the three evangelical counsels, confirmed by vow or other sacred bond," is also obliged to observe "a proper program of living [*ratio vivendi*] under his direction" (c. 603, §2). This kind of hermitess may be called "diocesan," in order to be distinguished from one in private vows or one who is a member of a monastery (cf. *CCEO*/1990, cc. 481–485). As this is the only canon in the 1983 Code which explicitly refers to the eremitic life, unless the *ratio vivendi* or particular law of the diocese provides norms governing the transfer of hermits (cf. *CCEO*/1990, c. 570), this question "must be resolved in light of laws issued in similar matters" (c. 19). Since the form of consecrated life most similar to the eremitic life is that of consecrated virgins,[2] four paragraphs from the recent

---

[1] United Nations, General Assembly, *Universal Declaration of Human Rights*, art. 13, 10 December 1948, https://www.un.org/en/universal-declaration-human-rights/index.html (accessed 6 March 2020) [hereafter *UDHR*].

[2] See, generally, C.M. Hip-Flores, *Hermits and Consecrated Virgins, Ancient Vocations in the Contemporary Catholic Church: A Canonical-Pastoral Study of Canons 603 and 604 Individual Forms of Consecrated Life* (Christina Hip-Flores, 2018); J.M. Stegman, "'Mystically Espoused to Christ, the Son of God (c. 604 §1)': The Basis for Proposing Juridic Principles to Guide the Development of Norms for the *Ordo virginum*," Washington, DC, Catholic University of America, 2019; see also S.O. Sheridan, "Consecrated Virgins and Hermits," in *The Jurist*, 73 (2013), 493–512.

instruction *Ecclesiae sponsae imago*[3] (*ESI*) may be helpfully consulted, *mutatis mutandis*.

In the first place, *ESI* establishes that:

> Although [public profession of the evangelical counsels] establishes a special insertion in the particular Church in which it is [made], it does not prevent [hermits] from transferring to another particular Church, if necessary, either permanently or on a temporary basis: for example, for employment, family, or pastoral purposes, or for other reasonable and proportionate motives.[4]

This paragraph generally applies to hermits, but not in every respect. For example, although it is true that hermits "devote their life to the praise of God and the salvation of the world through a stricter withdrawal from the world, the silence of solitude, and assiduous prayer and penance" (c. 603, §1), since most hermits today are likely to be self-supporting, transfers for the sake of an employment more in accord with their charism should be granted. It does not seem fitting, however, for a hermit to transfer for the sake of "pastoral purposes"—if this phrase is taken to mean "active works of the apostolate"—since this is not in conformity with the eremitic charism. A hermit may, however, legitimately request a transfer in order to receive more beneficial pastoral care.

Secondly, *ESI* continues:

> If a [hermitess] intends to transfer permanently to another diocese, she will explain her reasons to her own bishop, who will give her his opinion on the proposal. She can then ask the bishop of the diocese *ad quem* for [permission]. The latter, having received an introduction of the [hermitess] from the bishop of the diocese *a quo*, giving the reasons for the transfer and his own opinion, will make his decision and communicate his response to the applicant. He will also inform the bishop of the diocese *a quo*. If the response is positive, the bishop of the diocese *ad quem* will accept the [hermitess and] present her to his particular Church. . . . He will arrange with her what will be necessary and useful for her personal situation. Based on an evaluation, the bishop of the diocese *ad quem* can also refuse to accept her or, with the

---

[3] CICLSAL, instruction on the *Ordo consecrationis virginum* of 1970 *Ecclesiae sponsae imago*, 8 June 2018, *AAS* 110 (2018) 1042–1095, http://www.vatican.va/roman_curia/congregations/ccscrlife/documents/rc_con_ccscrlife_doc_20180608_istruzione-ecclesiaesponsaeimago_en.html (accessed 5 March 2020) [hereafter *ESI*].

[4] Ibid., 60.

agreement of the bishop of the diocese *a quo*, can fix a time of probation. In this case, while maintaining her link with the diocese *a quo*, the [hermitess] can nevertheless transfer her canonical domicile to the diocese *ad quem*, abiding by the guidelines agreed with both bishops concerning her personal situation.[5]

Naturally, one of the first things a receiving bishop will wish to do is to review the *ratio vivendi* and meet with the applicant. Prudence dictates that the bishop should also require the applicant to submit to the same vetting process required of visiting clergy or religious. The bishop may also wish to inquire as to the means support for the hermitess. The instruction does not elaborate on the procedure to be followed if either bishop's decision is unfavorable. In that case, if either bishop decides not to permit the transfer, he must issue this decree in writing and communicate it to the applicant, "with the reasons at least summarily expressed" (c. 51). If the applicant considers herself aggrieved by the decree from her own bishop (*a quo*), she may take recourse according to canons 1732–1739. Such recourse, since it does not concern a judicial sentence or decree which imposes or declares a penalty, does not have a suspensive effect (cf. c. 1353). Although the applicant might wish to challenge an unfavorable decision from the bishop *ad quem*, since that bishop has no *obligation* to receive her, she has no *right* to be received; thus, such a *libellus* would most likely be rejected *in limine* due to its lack of foundation (c. 1505 §2, 4°).[6]

Thirdly, after a favorable evaluation or suitable time of probation, *ESI* provides the following:

> Personally or through a delegate, the bishop will take care to inform the [diocese] in an appropriate way about the temporary or definitive transfer of a [hermitess] to another diocese, and also about the acceptance of a [hermitess] from another diocese.[7]

Since the temporary or definitive transfer of a hermitess is a public juridic act, it needs to be documented and published in a manner suitable to the particular Church in question. In most dioceses of the United States, for example, publication could fittingly be done by means of the diocesan newspaper, as well as in the parish bulletins of the deanery in which the hermitess is to reside. This

---

[5] *ESI* 62.

[6] On this precise point, see W.L. Daniel, "Rejection of a *libellus* Due to the Lack of Any Foundation Whatsoever," in *Studia canonica* 43 (2009) 361–387.

[7] *ESI* 63.

would have the positive effects of welcoming the hermitess to her new domicile as well as avoiding any possible wonderment on the part of the faithful.

Fourthly, it would seem fitting for the diocesan bishop to keep a register of hermits, as is now required by *ESI* for consecrated virgins.

> After the [public profession] has taken place, it will be documented with an entry in the register of [hermits], adding the personal signature of the celebrating minister, the [hermitess] herself and two witnesses. This register is ordinarily safeguarded in the diocesan curia. A certificate of the event will be issued to the [hermitess]. It is also appropriate for the bishop to make arrangements to inform the competent parish priest about the [profession] so that it can be annotated in the baptismal register.[8]

This would be of great practical help to the parish priest who wishes, for example, to verify the juridic status of a *peregrina* or *vaga* presenting herself as a diocesan hermitess.

Finally, the existence of a probable *lacuna legis* should be noted. As pointed out by Christina Hip-Flores,[9] although "a public perpetual vow of chastity [made] *in a religious institute*" (c. 1088) is a diriment impediment to marriage, the same vow made by a hermit (or consecrated virgin) is not. This author agrees with Judith Stegman, *inter alios*, that this *lacuna* ought to be addressed in a future revision of the law.[10]

Rev. Brian T. Austin, FSSP, JCD, PhD

---

[8] *ESI* 107.
[9] Hip-Flores, *Hermits and Consecrated Virgins*, loc. 404.
[10] Stegman, "Mystically Espoused to Christ," 212–216.

CANON 636

FINANCE OFFICER IN A RELIGIOUS INSTITUTE

With the decline of vocations to religious life, canonists are frequently asked if a general/provincial finance officer must be a member of the institute.

OPINION

Canon 636 provides for a finance officer but does not state that the person must be a member of the institute. However, each religious institute must follow the norms in the constitutions and directory/statutes of its proper law. In some instances, institutes provide that the finance officer be a member of the institute in the constitutions; still other institutes provide for the same in the directory/statutes. In such cases, changes cannot be made in the constitutions unless there is a two-third vote of the general chapter and the approval of the Congregation for Institutes of Consecrated Life and Societies of Apostolic Life (CICLSAL) for institutes of pontifical right institute. Diocesan bishops where the principal houses of diocesan right institutes are located can grant the change. Changes in the directory/statutes of institutes can be made by a two-third vote of the general chapter (c. 587 §2, §4).

A few years ago, consultors to CICLSAL were asked for their opinions regarding canon 636, i.e., if the finance officer had to be a member of the religious institute. A consultor, at that time, this canonist reviewed the 1917 Code of Canon Law and the present 1983 Code of Canon Law only to discover that neither code stated that the finance officer had to be a member of the institute. After sending her opinion to CICLSAL, she discussed the issue with another consultor at the CLSA Convention. He held the same opinion, i.e., that a non-member could be the finance officer. However, there has never been any directive from the said congregation regarding the finance officer of a religious institute.

Today, major superiors often have no member with financial expertise to fulfill that office. In such cases, this canonist advises that, while awaiting a general chapter to address the issue, a member knowledgeable regarding the patrimony of the institute (c. 578) be named as finance officer in accord with the proper law of the institute. A non-member (cleric, religious from another institute, or lay person) with expertise in financial affairs should be employed by the institute to serve as Director of Finance/Temporal Goods or some such title to administer the finances of the institute. The religious familiar with the patrimony of the institute offers invaluable service because the person with financial expertise may think he or she is there to make a profit for the religious institute. The temporal goods of religious institutes, public juridic persons, are ecclesiastical goods (c. 1257), and they must be used in accord with the proper purposes (c. 1254 §2). Religious institutes have a right to acquire, retain, administer and alienate such temporal goods in accord with Book V of the Code of Canon Law and the nature, purpose, spirit and character of the institute (cc. 1255, 578). The person appointed as the Director of Finance or Temporal Goods fulfills his/her function under the direction of the respective superior (c. 636 §1).

Rose McDermott, SSJ

Canon 668

Relatives Raising Questions Regarding a Sister's Inheritance

Our law firm began working with the estate of an extremely wealthy family some time ago. One of the heirs is a nun. Her relatives fear that her community will get all of her inheritance when she dies. This understanding comes from their pastor. If this is true, the relatives will contest it in civil court. Three of our civil lawyers are working on the estate issues. None of us are Catholics. We know next to nothing about canon law. Is it true that this nun's community gets her share of the inheritance regardless of her wishes?

Opinion

Canon 668 regulates the practical expression of the obligations assumed with the evangelical counsel of poverty as described in canon 600. It distinguishes between the personal property[1] of the individual religious and income generated by the individual but belonging to the religious institute. It is a canon that encourages simplicity, communal sharing, and detachment.

The first paragraph provides for religious who, by virtue of their Constitutions and other supplementary internal documents[2] are allowed to own personal property. The canon lists three very important items: (1) cession of administration of property, (2) disposition of the use of property including revenue (sometimes referred to as usufruct), and (3) a will. Even though the canon does not require that (1) and (2) be done through a civil document, it is advisable that they be carried out in such a way, particularly if the value of the property is substantial.

The religious may designate a family member, a law firm, the religious institute or someone else to administer the property. When (1) and (2) are given to an individual or an entity other than the religious institute, a durable power of attorney or a trust vehicle will need to be used. Once cession of administration is

---

[1] The Code uses the term patrimony to refer to the property and monies of an individual religious. Civil law uses the term assets. Any canons referenced in this opinion are from *Code of Canon Law, Latin-English Edition: New English Translation* (Washington, DC: Canon Law Society of America, 2012).

[2] The constitutions and other supplementary law within the religious institute are known as proper law. This differs from particular law such as the law of the diocese or universal law which refers to the Code of Canon Law. There are also other categories of laws.

accomplished, the religious should have *no further involvement* with the property and its revenue. A trust exists for this particular sister, and it has been reviewed by this author.[3]

The third component, a will, must be in place at least before perpetual profession, whether or not the member owns any personal property. The will must conform to civil law requirements. When the member retains ownership of her assets, the distribution of the assets in the will may be to *whomever she wishes unless the proper law of the institute states otherwise.*

Once the three items in the initial paragraph of this canon are in place, a religious *may not alter them without permission.* Therefore, while the second paragraph provides for changing the documents that are already in place as well as placing other acts regarding temporal goods, it rightly places a great deal of importance on the relationship that the member has with the institute. The authority to permit the change rests with the superior competent according to the proper law of the religious institute. Any just cause will be sufficient reason to grant the permission. Just cause is normally interpreted very broadly to include any reasonable request, e.g., a family need, change in the administrator due to health, assuming power of attorney for an ailing parent, acting as an executor of a will, something missing in the original document and, perhaps, some need which has come to the attention of the individual religious. Permission must be given *before* changes are made and *not after* something has already been executed. The change should be done in writing and retained in the member's file.

The third paragraph of this canon deals with those items that *are not* the personal property of the religious. Once the person has professed vows, anything the member acquires *as a result of her ministry* belongs to the institute. Examples are: pension, salary, bonuses, royalties, insurance settlements, lottery winnings, death benefits and social security. An exception includes pensions or other benefits accruing to a religious from employment prior to admission into the institute. Inheritances received from family members, remain personal property, but other legacies, bequests or gifts are normally the property of the religious institute. When there is doubt regarding the facts of the situation or the intention of the benefactor, the gifts are considered belonging to the institute in accordance with canon 1267 §1.[4]

---

[3] Consultation with a knowledgeable civil lawyer is recommended.
[4] Canon 1267 §1 says: "Unless the contrary is established, offerings given to superiors or administrators of any ecclesiastical juridic person, even a private one, are presumed given to the juridic person itself."

The fourth and fifth paragraphs of this important canon pertain to institutes that by their very nature require members to completely renounce ownership of property. This requirement is specified in the proper law of the religious institute. Therefore, religious in this situation are canonically incapable of acquiring or owning property of any sort. Some institutes which do not require a member to renounce personal property do allow an individual religious to make such a decision sometime after profession of perpetual vows. If the member makes total renunciation, that person *must name the religious institute as the member's sole beneficiary*.

This author also reviewed the constitutions and supplementary documents of the particular congregation into which this religious has been incorporated through the profession of perpetual vows. She is a member of an apostolic institute of pontifical right. They are not a cloistered institute. The sisters profess simple rather than solemn vows.[5] It is crystal clear from these documents that this sister: (1) may retain ownership of patrimony and other goods she may acquire, (2) must renounce the individual administration of them, (3) freely determines the beneficiary of income received from her patrimony, and (4) makes a will that can only be changed with the permission of the congregation's superior general. In my conversations with the sister and her superior general, it is evident that a will has been in place for some time and that it conforms to civil law requirements.

The response to this question was followed by many more questions from these civil lawyers and the relatives. They included submitting two twenty-page papers about this matter. In the end the relatives, the superior general, the sister and the civil lawyers were very pleased with the outcome.[6] Careful consideration of all the issues as well as on-going, thought-provoking conversations were the ways to avoid a lawsuit.

Eileen Jaramillo, DMin, JCL

---

[5] Canon 1192 §2 is the only place in the Code that mentions solemn and simple vows. Orders having a long history such as Benedictines, Dominicans, Franciscans, Servites and Jesuits profess perpetual solemn vows while the more recent apostolic congregations profess simple vows. The difference from a juridical point of view is that religious who profess a solemn vow of poverty renounce ownership of all their temporal goods in accordance with canon 668 §§4-5. Congregations with simple vows adhere to canon 668 §1. It allows religious the right to retain ownership. However, religious must give up its use and any revenue.

[6] While the contents of those papers are confidential, the author recommends the following article to the reader: Rosemary Smith, "The Personal Patrimony of Individual Members of Religious Institutes: Current Issues," *CLSA Proceedings* 62 (2000) 263-281.

CIC 822, 212§3; CCEO 651, 15§3

WHEN CLERICS AND BISHOPS CLASH OVER WHAT CONSTITUTES APPROPRIATE USE OF SOCIAL MEDIA

Amplified in the world-wide COVID-19 pandemic, but already increasing year upon year, more and more attention by clergy is being marshalled to social media and blogging/Internet engagements. What canons and church teachings help us address growing disagreements between various clerics who are freely expressing their opinion on social media and web platforms vis-à-vis his Bishop's role of vigilance?[1]

OPINION

General Principles

Facebook launched February 4, 2004. Twitter launched July 15, 2006. Instagram, October 6, 2010. "Just Google it" and one readily finds these references online. The inception of online blogging was, however, a little more evolutionary in its roll-out. According to one historical account, what has become ubiquitously known as a blog began when links.net coined the term "weblog" in 1997, which subsequently was shortened to just "blog" in 1999; the term witnessed such rapid growth in usage and understanding that Merriam-Webster declared "blog" to be the break-out word of the year 2004.[2] Social media platforms and online presence, or in the language of the Church the means of social communications, continue to explode as even the sample listing noted above ignored less universally recognized ones added within the past decade.

---

[1] This opinion takes no position on any recently publicized cleric-bishop conflicts outside my diocesan experience as the facts, circumstances and record of those are completely unknown to the author canonist.

[2] Webdesigner Depot Staff, "A Brief History of Blogging," March 14, 2011, https://www.webdesignerdepot.com/2011/03/a-brief-history-of-blogging/ (accessed on 26 September 2020).

Our Church teaches that this, too, is mission territory.[3] Pope Francis, in his 2019 World Communications Day[4] (WCD) message, noted "today's media environment is so pervasive as to be indistinguishable from the sphere of everyday life. The Net is a resource of our time."[5] Eighteen years earlier, Pope John Paul II declared in his WCD evangelizing message, "Now we must proclaim that truth from the housetops. In today's world, housetops are almost always marked by a forest of transmitters and antennae sending and receiving messages of every kind to and from the four corners of the earth. It is vitally important to ensure that among these many messages the word of God is heard. To proclaim the faith from the housetops today means to speak Jesus' word in and through the dynamic world of communications."[6]

In 1975, Pope Paul VI in *Evangelii nuntiandi* stated:

> When they [mass media or means of social communications] are put at the service of the Gospel, they are capable of increasing almost indefinitely the area in which the Word of God is heard; they enable the Good News to reach millions of people. The Church would feel guilty before the Lord if she did not utilize these powerful means that human skill is daily rendering more perfect. It is through them that she proclaims 'from the housetops' the message of which she is the depositary. In them she finds a modern and effective version of the pulpit. Thanks to them she succeeds in speaking to the multitudes.[7]

---

[3] Cf. Vatican Council II, *Inter Mirifica (IM)* 3; Pope Paul VI, *Evangelii Nuntiandi* (EN) 45, http://www.vatican.va/content/paul-vi/en/apost_exhortations/documents/hf_p-vi_exh_ 19751208_evangelii-nuntiandi.html (accessed on 25 September 2020; Pope John Paul II, *Redemptoris Missio* 37; Pontifical Council for Social Communications, *Communio et Progressio* (CeP), 126-134; [Author], *Aetatis Novae* (AN) 11.

[4] The only annual day mandated by the Council Fathers of the Second Vatican Council; see IM 18.

[5] Pope Francis, "Message of His Holiness Pope Francis for the 53rd World Communications Day" 2, 24 January 2019, http://www.vatican.va/content/francesco/ en/messages/communications/documents/papa-francesco_20190124_messaggio-comunic azioni-sociali.html (accessed on 25 September 2020).

[6] Pope John Paul II, "Message of The Holy Father John Paul II for the 35th World Communications Day" 1, January 24, 2001 http://www.vatican.va/content/ john-paul-ii/en/messages/communications/documents/hf_jp-ii_mes_20010124_world-communicati ons-day.html (accessed on 25 September 2020).

[7] EN 45.

A final brief illustration of the Church's understanding of the vast importance of social media and the Internet, the *Directory for the Pastoral Ministry of Bishop* declares:

[F]ollowing the example of Saint Paul (cf. Acts 17), the Church seeks to spread the message of salvation through the "new Areopagi" in which culture is defined and disseminated, especially through the communications media. These include periodicals and journals, television, radio, cinema and, increasingly, internet and information technology.[8]

Means of Social Communication

CIC Canon 822 §1: The pastors of the Church, using a right proper to the Church in fulfilling their function, are to endeavor to make use of the instruments of social communication.

§2. These same pastors are to take care to teach the faithful that they are bound by the duty of cooperating so that a human and Christian spirit enlivens the use of instruments of social communication.

CCEO Canon 651 §1: In order to fulfill its function of announcing the gospel throughout the world, the Church is bound to make use of appropriate means. Therefore, it is necessary to vindicate everywhere the right to the use of the means of social communication and specifically to the freedom of the press.

§2. All the Christian faithful for their part are to collaborate in this great mission of the church, and support and foster the initiatives of this apostolate.

It is no surprise, then, that clerics, and particularly priests as pastors and in other evangelizing ministry roles, utilize the world wide web and other social communications technology to get one's message and mission, opinion and opus to an everyday audience, to both housetops and mobile devices.

A two-way flow of information and views between pastors and faithful, freedom of expression sensitive to the well-being of the community and to the role of the Magisterium in fostering it, and responsible public

---

[8] Congregation for Bishops, *Apostolorum successores* 137, February 22, 2004, http://www.vatican.va/roman_curia/congregations/cbishops/documents/rc_con_cbishops_ doc_20040222_apostolorum-successores_en.html#Chapter_VI (accessed on 25 September 2020).

opinion all are important expressions of 'the fundamental right of dialogue and information within the Church' (*Aetatis Novae*, 10; cf. *Communio et Progressio*, 20).[9]

Priests and deacons and bishops are most often effectively using Facebook, Twitter, Instagram, blogs, YouTube, LinkedIn, and so many other media technologies to speak a word, speak the Word of Jesus Christ to their parish, their apostolate, their (arch)diocese, actually to the entire world. These good endeavors are to be commended—and where able, expanded. Still, there exist occasional areas of tensions among the ordained.

Rights and Duties of the Priest and Deacon

Often it is forgotten that the canonical rights and duties of the members of the Christian faithful stipulated in canons 208-223 belong also to clerics. Priests and deacons have the right to express their "opinion on matters which pertain to the good of the Church and to make their opinions known to the rest of the Christian faithful." [10] The cleric's opinion, like others, is to be an informed opinion. This informed opinion is not one restricted, however, to the content of the written or oral composition alone or to the correct context of a picture or video. This opinion is also to be formed, shaped and educated vis-à-vis two additional principal factors: a) the format structure (or modality) of that particular or similar social media transmission and b) knowledge on how the particular communication authored by the cleric will potentially be received by others.

Officially since 1986, priests during their years of seminary formation[11] are to be trained on the use of the means of social communications. Admittedly, seminaries

---

[9] Pontifical Council for Social Communication, "Ethics in Communication" 26, June 4, 2000, http://www.vatican.va/roman_curia/pontifical_councils/pccs/documents/rc_pc_ pcc s_doc_20000530_ethics-communications_en.html (accessed on 25 September 2020).
[10] CIC c. 212 §3: "According to the knowledge, competence and prestige which they possess, they have the right and even at times the duty to manifest to the sacred pastors their opinion on matters which pertain to the good of the Church and to make their opinion known to the rest of the Christian faithful, without prejudice to the integrity of faith and morals, with reverence toward their pastors, and attentive to common advantage and the dignity of persons." CCEO canon 15§3: "In keeping with their knowledge, competence and position, they have the right and at times even the duty, to manifest their views on matters regarding the good of the Church to the pastors of the Church and also to other Christian faithful, with due regard for the integrity of faith and morals and respect toward the same pastors, with consideration for the common benefit and the dignity of persons."
[11] Congregation for Catholic Education, Guide to the Training of Future Priests Concerning the Instruments of Social Communication, March 19, 1985, 68: "Since people in today's culture are trained and regulated not only by books and teachers, but in even

like society in general, can no longer keep up with the vastly changing technology. Nevertheless they can and ought within their curricula to have an in-depth course on "media literacy education"[12] which has been required at varying levels by the Church since at least the 1936 encyclical *Vigilanti cura* of Pope Pius IX specifically addressing the teaching influence of motion pictures or the movies. Today, "the Pastors of the Church need to know how to make use of these media in accomplishing their mission, realizing how effective they can be for the spread of the Gospel."[13] For the sake of the Gospel, a four-fold media literacy framework to access, to analyze, to evaluate and to create,[14] assists all the Christian faithful in one's responsibility in engagement of the means of social communication.

During the Rite of Ordination, the Deacon, now a new cleric receives the Book of the Gospels: "Receive the Gospel of Christ, whose herald you have become. Believe what you read, teach what you believe, and practice what you teach."[15] Clerics teach their belief in their postings and tweets, their likes and sharings, their video production and other media engagement. They "must take into account the common good of the Church, the rights of others, and their own duties toward others"[16] in fulfillment of proclaiming, heralding to the world on social media and the web. Likewise, clerics in cyberspace are not to "harm illegitimately the good reputation which a person possesses nor to injure the right of any person to protect his or her own privacy."[17] These engagements can be and most often are accomplished with great creativity, joy, dialogue and respect for human dignity.

However, one's creativity needs to be evaluated first and foremost by the cleric, not the local bishop. For example, is one's Twitter handle prudent? Could that

---

greater dependence on the audiovisual media, it is much to be desired that the priests shall know how to use these media well, that is, not passively giving in to them, but capable of judging them critically. This, however, will be possible only if they are taught in the seminary by persons who are competent both in theory and practice, and if they are given exercises with these media, prudently and within reason, which will teach them how to discipline themselves, to educate the faithful, and to make effective use of the media in their apostolate." Cf. Pontifical Council for Social Communication, The Church and Internet, February 22, 2002, 11.

[12] Cf. Kenneth A. Riley, "For the Sake of the Gospel: The Implementation of Canon 822 With Respect to Media Literacy Education," JCL thesis, The Catholic University of America, 2004, specifically Chapter IV regarding seminarians but also youth, parents/teachers, elderly, media professionals among others. Cf. AN, 28; CeP 107; "Ethics in Communication" 25.

[13] AS 138. Cf. IM 3, 13; CIC cc. 747§1, 822§1.

[14] Cf. Riley, *For the Sake of the Gospel*, Chapter II.

[15] The Roman Pontifical, "Rite of Ordination of One Deacon," (2011) 238.

[16] CIC c. 223 §1; CCEO c. 26 §1.

[17] CIC c. 220; CCEO c. 23.

handle be considered vain[18] or grooming or misunderstood in the culture of misconduct—adult or minor? Are one's Facebook posts or similar social media output "fostering the peace and harmony based on justice which are to be observed among people"?[19] Justice is key and occasionally demands harsh but true words, but always words conveyed with charity.[20] The USCCB "Social Media Guidelines"[21] regarding visibility, community and accountability issues and values, even though composed for parishes, schools and Catholic institutions, are nonetheless helpful for a cleric's careful consideration.

Canon 212 concludes noting that the right to share an informed opinion is modified: one "without prejudice to the integrity of faith and morals, with reverence toward their pastors, and attentive to common advantage and the dignity of persons."[22]

Rights and Duties of the Bishop

The vigilance[23] of the means of social communication by Bishops was decreed in *Inter Mirifica*: "It will be the task of the Bishops, however, to watch over such works [all media of social communication, including the press] and undertakings in their own dioceses, to promote them and, as far as the public apostolate is concerned, to guide them, not excluding those that are under the direction of exempt religious."[24] While the CIC solely delineates books within canons 824-830 and other writings more broadly within canons 831-832, the *mens legislatoris* and Church teaching is evidenced more expansively seven years later in CCEO canon 654: "The norms of common law on books apply also to any other writings

---

[18] CIC c. 282 §1.

[19] CIC c. 287§1; CCEO c. 384.

[20] A few varied examples of guidelines for posting of comments and engagement include: https://thedeaconsbench.com/about/guidelines-for-comments/;

https://www.patheos.com/blogs/theanchoress/comment-policy/;

https://www.catholic.com/magazine/print-edition/the-donts-and-dos-of-the-catholic-blogosphere (all websites accessed on September 25, 2020).

[21] United States Conference of Catholic Bishops, "Social Media Guidelines," http://www.usccb.org/about/communications/social-media-guidelines.cfm (accessed on September 25, 2020).

[22] CIC c. 212§3; CCEO c. 26 §2.

[23] Cf. CIC cc. 392, 823; CCEO c. 201; Congregation for the Doctrine of the Faith, Instruction, "*Donum veritatis* On the Ecclesial Vocation of the Theologian" 20, May 24, 1990: "The pastoral task of the Magisterium is one of vigilance. It seeks to ensure that the People of God remain in the truth which sets free. It is therefore a complex and diversified reality. The theologian, to be faithful to his role of service to the truth, must take into account the proper mission of the Magisterium and collaborate with it."

[24] IM 20.

or messages whatever reproduced by any technical means and intended for public distribution."[25] Social media and blogging posts, for example, are publicly distributed. That is their *raison d'être*.

Because of the duty of vigilance, bishops will sometimes need to intervene, perhaps even to a level of penalizing or sanctioning, by applying CIC canon 1369 or CCEO canon 652 §2 as a last resort.

> In the context of their duty to watch over the deposit of faith and preserve it intact (cf. can. 386 and 747, §1) and to satisfy the faithful's right to guidance in the way of sound doctrine (cf. can. 213 and 317), the Bishops also have the right and duty to: a) "be vigilant lest harm be done to the faith or morals of the Christian faithful through writings or the use of the instruments of social communication" (c. 823, §1); . . . c) "denounce writings which harm correct faith or good morals" (c. 823, §1); and d) apply, as the case requires, those administrative and penal sanctions provided for in the Church's law to those who by infringement of the canonical norms abuse their proper office, constitute a danger to ecclesiastical communion, or do harm to the faith and morals of the faithful (cf. can. 805; 810 §1; 194 §1, n. 2; 1369; 1371 1º; 1389).[26]

Conclusion

However, sanctions and penalties are unlikely to resolve satisfactorily the growing disagreements as expressed in our presenting question between clerics and bishops. Before these are imposed, a more robust dialogue of issues and concerns would be most beneficial and paternally appropriate for a Bishop as Father to his priests and deacons. Helpful and useful, too, is for the Bishop or his delegate to delineate particular concerns in a written form.[27] Admittedly, however, there ought to be some guarantee that the document of the local chancery leader will not become exhibit A on the cleric's next posting or public distribution, one potentially inflaming any disagreement further. Prudence demands navigating this minefield with the assistance of other persons of good will.

---

[25] CCEO c. 654.

[26] Congregation for the Doctrine of the Faith, "Instruction on Some Aspects of the Use of the Instruments of Social Communication in Promoting the Doctrine of the Faith" 2, March 30, 1992, http://www.vatican.va/roman_curia/congregations/cfaith/documents/rc_con_cfaith_doc_19920330_istruzione-pccs_en.html (accessed on September 25, 2020). Cf. AS 140.

[27] CIC cc. 50-51; CCEO cc. 1517, 1514, 1519.

Likewise, as both Bishop and cleric engage in dialogue regarding potential disagreements in this important area of social communications, a published diocesan pastoral plan[28] would prove to be an invaluable resource regarding the means of social communications that includes procedures and protocols on how-to address perceived disagreements regarding a cleric's publicly distributed statements, posts, opinions, and insights. Application of such a plan will aid both the priest or deacon and his bishop in truly using the means of social communications for the salvation of souls, the real communication that matters.

Very Reverend Kenneth A. Riley, JCL

---

[28] AN, 24 a-f, 10; Cf. AS 138. The plan would be for (arch)diocesan and parish employees, too.

The Right to the Sacraments During a Pandemic

Can a dying person be denied Penance, Anointing of the Sick, Viaticum or the Apostolic pardon, commonly known as the "last rites" of the Catholic Church? During the COVID-19 pandemic numerous reports surfaced of the Catholic faithful being denied the sacraments by hospitals due to the contagious nature of the virus. Creative methods to respect the rights of persons, including the dying, to the sacraments emerged raising questions of validity. At least one archdiocese developed a cadre of infection-control-trained priests willing to engage in such a ministry, while establishing a separate residence for such teams of priests to minimize COVID spread. Some diocesan bishops, reportedly during the COVID-19 pandemic, restricted access to sacraments such as Penance and Anointing of the Sick.[1] However, Canon 213 states; "The Christian faithful have the right to receive assistance from the sacred pastors out of the spiritual goods of the Church, especially the word of God and the sacraments." Furthermore Canon 843 §1. states "Sacred ministers cannot deny the sacraments to those who seek them at appropriate times, are properly disposed, and are not prohibited by law from receiving them."[2]

Opinion

Catholics have become more aware of the need for the sacraments when they became unavailable during the COVID-19 pandemic. The local bishops, working with public health authorities, have been reviewing the issue of what constitutes "appropriate times" during this pandemic, with emphasis on protecting the individual parishioner, the congregation, the general public, and the ministers of the sacraments. While consistent with canon 838 §4, the diocesan bishop has the authority to "to issue liturgical norms which bind everyone" in the Church

---

[1]   J.D. Flynn, "Mass. bishop 'suspends' sacramental anointing while rescinding controversial policy," *Catholic News Service* (March 27, 2020), https://www.catholic newsagency.com/news/mass-bishop-suspends-sacramental-anointing-while-rescinding-controversial-policy-19344 (accessed on 2 October 2020); Terry Mattingly, "No confessions? Coronavirus crisis creates legal, doctrinal Lenten minefield for priests," *Get Religion* (April 7, 2020), https://www.getreligion.org/getreligion/2020/4/6/coronavirus-crisis-creates-a-legal-doctrinal-lenten-minefield-for-priests-and-their-flocks (accessed on 2 October 2020).

[2]   All citations from canons have been taken from *Code of Canon Law: Latin-English Translation* (Washington, DC: Canon Law Society of America, 1999).

entrusted to his care, such regulations cannot be contradictory to canon and liturgical laws promulgated by the Apostolic See.[3] Consistent with canon 1752 ultimately the purpose of all canon law is for the salvation of souls. Thus, every restriction on the access to the sacraments must respect the precedence of canon 213, citing the right of the faithful "to receive assistance from the sacred pastors out of the spiritual goods of the Church, especially the word of God and the sacraments," as well as canon 843 §1: "Sacred ministers cannot deny the sacraments to those who seek them at appropriate times, are properly disposed, and are not prohibited by law from receiving them." It is clear, during the pandemic the faithful have been denied access to the sacraments. This has been particularly morally harmful for those who are dying. Furthermore, loved ones may not have access to their ill family members at such a vulnerable time. Even when requesting sacraments for their dying loved ones, there is no guarantee that clergy will have direct access to the dying. Thus, at many levels, the hunger for the sacraments continues, and harm is being imposed.

Perhaps the most urgent matter is access to the sacraments of Penance and Anointing of the Sick as well as to the Apostolic pardon. Considering these challenges, the Apostolic Penitentiary recently issued provisions for special indulgences and addressed collective, or general, absolution during the COVID-19 pandemic.

The Sacrament of Penance

There is no more applicable canon than 978 §1: "In hearing confessions the priest is to remember that he is equally a judge and a physician and has been established by God as a minister of divine justice and mercy, so that he has regard for the divine honor and the salvation of souls." Canon law dictates not just who can forgive sins, but also the place for it to occur: "The proper place to hear sacramental confessions is a church or oratory. The conference of bishops is to establish norms regarding the confessional; it is to take care, however, that there are always confessionals with a fixed grate between the penitent and the confessor in an open place so that the faithful who wish to can use them freely. Confessions are not to be heard outside a confessional without a just cause" (can. 964 §§1-2; see also can. 967 §§1-3). But regardless of some bishops restricting scheduled confessions, even outdoor confessions due to "shelter in place" orders by secular

---

[3] C. 838 §1: "The direction of the sacred liturgy depends solely on the authority of the Church which resides in the Apostolic See and, according to the norm of law, the diocesan bishop."

authorities, the faithful have a right to the sacraments, especially Penance, so critical to the salvation of souls.

Penance and Social Distancing

The pandemic clearly would equate to a just cause for confessions to be heard outside of a confessional. Social distancing and even quarantine are necessary to protect not only the priest but also the penitent. A number of priests have developed creative ways to respect confidentiality, the sacrament, and the health of all involved. Some priests have engaged in outdoor "parking lot" confessions in which the penitent sits in the car (of course, only one person per car), and the priest sits at a prescribed distance from the car window, with a confessional screen placed so the identity of the penitent is protected. Traffic control agents are placed to ensure proper distance between cars. At least one diocesan bishop had prohibited this. It would be prudent to seek the permission of one's local diocesan bishop, consistent with canon 838 §1 cited above, as well as canon 835 §1: "The bishops in the first place exercise the sanctifying function; they are the high priests, the principal dispensers of the mysteries of God, and the directors, promoters, and guardians of the entire liturgical life in the church entrusted to them." However, the bishop needs to weigh judiciously the exercise of such authority, consistent with the right of the faithful to the sacraments. The local health department also should be contacted, for example, with questions about the danger of droplet contagion due to the manner in which confessions are heard. However, they should have no authority over how and when sacraments are administered, especially if interfering with the right of the faithful to the sacraments. The Church's Apostolic Penitentiary has identified prudential measures for celebrating Penance, including "the celebration in a ventilated place outside the confessional, the adoption of a suitable distance, the use of protective masks, without prejudice to absolute attention to the safeguarding of the sacramental seal and the necessary discretion."[4]

But what about vulnerable individuals who are unable to travel: those in hospitals, hospices, or nursing homes without a Catholic chaplain? Creative alternatives have been proposed. In cases of grave necessity, the diocesan bishop may determine that it is lawful to impart general absolution, as described by the Apostolic Penitentiary, "for example, at the entrance to hospital wards, where the infected faithful in danger of death are hospitalised, using as far as possible and

---

[4]   Apostolic Penitentiary, "Note on the Sacrament of Reconciliation in the current pandemic" (March 20, 2020) https://press.vatican.va/content/salastampa/en/bollettino/pub blico/2020/03/20/200320d.html (accessed on 2 October 2020), available on page 63 of this publication.

with the appropriate precautions the means of amplifying the voice so that absolution may be heard."[5] One priest indicated that his local bishop has approved his use of a bullhorn outside of a nursing home to impart general absolution. Perhaps with the permission of the diocesan bishop, this could even be followed by the Apostolic pardon.

General Absolution

While individual confession is the ordinary way of celebrating the sacrament of Penance (can. 960), general absolution can be imparted under certain circumstance. The first scenario is when there is an imminent danger of death, and there is insufficient time for the priest or priests to hear the confessions of the individual penitents. The second scenario is when there is grave necessity—that is, when there are not enough confessors available to hear the confessions of the number of individuals, and thus persons will be deprived of the sacrament for a long while (The United States Conference of Catholic Bishops/USCCB has determined this to be one month.) The diocesan bishop determines if the conditions of a grave necessity are present, consistent with criteria of the USCCB (can. 961 §§1–2). The Apostolic Penitentiary believes that, especially in the places most affected by the pandemic and until the phenomenon recedes, the cases of serious need will occur. If a sudden need exists for collective absolution, the priest is obliged to warn the diocesan bishop. If the priest cannot do so, he should inform the bishop as soon as possible. However, this obligation to report after the fact to the diocesan bishop was removed from the ritual.[6]

For general absolution to be valid, the penitent must be properly disposed, and intend to confess serious sins within a suitable period of time (can. 962 §1).[7] In 1974 the National Conference of Catholic Bishops issued a decree requiring some external sign of contrition with the use of General absolution: "appropriate external sign of penance to be shown, e.g., kneeling, bowing of head, bowing deeply, standing (if the penitents have been kneeling), a gesture such as the sign of the cross, etc."[8] Canon 963 cites the obligation to approach individual confession "as soon as possible; given the opportunity, before receiving another

---

[5] Ibid.

[6] Frederick R. McManus, "Title IV: The Sacrament of Penance," *New Commentary on the Code of Canon Law*, eds. John P. Beal, James A. Coriden, and Thomas J. Green (Mahwah, NJ: Paulist Press, 2000) 1146.

[7] C. 987: "To receive the salvific remedy of the sacrament of penance, a member of the Christian faithful must be disposed in such a way that, rejecting sins committed and having a purpose of amendment, the person is turned back to God."

[8] Committee on the Liturgy, *Bishops' Committee on the Liturgy Newsletter 1965-1975* (Washington, DC: National Conference of Catholic Bishops, 1974) 450.

general absolution, unless a just cause intervenes." The Apostolic Penitentiary uses the term "in due time." Insofar as it can be done, the penitent is to be instructed on this obligation and exhorted to make an act of contrition before absolution if there is time (can. 962 §§1–2).

Rite for Emergencies

Increasingly there are situations in which a priest is called to hear Confession and provide Anointing of the Sick for a gravely ill patient for whom direct and private access is prohibited. In this situation, the priest is physically present to the patient but remotely so—such as standing outside a patient's room—where confidentiality will be breached. Canon law dictates that "individual and integral confession and absolution constitute the only ordinary means by which a member of the faithful conscious of grave sin is reconciled with God and the Church. *Only physical or moral impossibility excuses from confession of this type; in such a case reconciliation can be obtained by other means*" (can. 960, emphasis added). The roles of the diocesan bishop and the USCCB in determining situations in which those impossibilities exist is less clear. But the Rite for Emergencies provides guidance for "when the danger of death from injury or illness is sudden and unexpected or when a priest is not called to exercise his ministry until the person is at the point of death."[9] It indicates that if necessary the confession of sins may be generic.

Possible Scenarios During a Pandemic

In the first scenario, the priest is able to get access to Personal Protective Equipment (PPE)[10] and professional supervision of its use necessary to enable a physical presence to the patient. Essential in all of these scenarios are the use of a protective mask and protective gloves. The confessional stole, if used, should be completely under the PPE. In this case Penance (depending on the circumstances, either an individual and integral confession, or confession in a generic way as in the Rite for Emergencies), the Anointing of the Sick, and the Apostolic pardon (both addressed below) can be administered. It even may be possible to give Viaticum, if no pyx is opened in the patient's room. It should not be brought into the room unless it remains secured under PPE. Nothing that cannot be discarded in the patient room should be brought into the room. Formulas for any of the

---

[9] International Commission on English in the Liturgy, *Pastoral Care of the Sick: Rites of Anointing and Viaticum* (Collegeville, MN: ICEL, 2004) n. 259.

[10] Personal Protective Equipment (PPE) is a phrase used by the federal government and defined as "equipment worn to minimize exposure to hazards that cause serious workplace injuries and illnesses." See, e.g., https://www.osha.gov/personal-protective-equipment (accessed on 27 September 2020).

sacraments or blessings can be written on a disposable card (to be disposed of in the patient's room). It is also important to seek direction, beforehand, from the patient's health personnel about standards for not introducing pathogens into the patient's environment when bringing to the patient Holy Eucharist and the Oil of the Sick. The use of host, oils, and their receptables that have had direct or indirect contact with other persons must be prevented. The priest must follow strict protocol for entering and exiting the room, as directed by the health personnel. The Apostolic Penitentiary also has recommended that bishops consider establishing agreements with local health authorities for groups of "extraordinary hospital chaplains … in compliance with the norms of protection from contagion, to guarantee the necessary spiritual assistance to the sick and dying."[11] The Archdiocese of Boston successfully has developed such a ministry.[12] Again, there is the option for general absolution as described by the Apostolic Penitentiary or the Rite for Emergencies that involves no direct contact.

In the second scenario, the priest is able to communicate directly with the patient from a short distance, while looking through a window, or in or just outside of a doorway (either speaking loudly or through an amplifying device) but cannot have physical closeness with the person. In that case, the Rite for Emergencies and the Apostolic pardon would be possible, but administration of anointing would not be possible. Obviously, due to the seal of confession there can be no articulation of sins. In this scenario, the requirements for absolution include an expression of sorrow and the intention to confess serious sins within a suitable period of time, as also referenced for general absolution. The priest can ask the patient to say, if possible, that he is sorry for any sins that may have been committed, indicating that at a suitable period of time if any unconfessed serious sins exist, they are to be confessed. While the priest should see some sign of contrition, when the patient is unable to demonstrate such a sign to the priest, and Anointing of the Sick is impossible, conditional absolution may be administered. However, the advantage of the Anointing of the Sick, over the Rite for Emergencies, is that there is no need for the priest to receive an external sign of contrition required for absolution, for example with an unconscious patient. This all assumes that health care personnel have approved the access required and there is compliance with their hygienic directives.

---

[11] Apostolic Penitentiary, "Note on the Sacrament of Reconciliation."

[12] Caroline Enos, "Catholic priests anoint 1,100 COVID-19 patients in eastern Mass. during pandemic," *Boston Globe* (July 10, 2020), https://www.bostonglobe.com/2020/07/02/metro/catholic-priests-give-last-rights-1100-covid-19-patients-eastern-mass-during-pandemic/ (accessed on 27 September 2020).

In the third scenario, the priest cannot have any direct presence to the person. When it is impossible to receive sacramental absolution, one should not forget that it is possible to obtain forgiveness of sin, even mortal sins, by expressing perfect contrition coming from one's love of God. It must be accompanied by the firm resolution to have recourse as soon as possible to sacramental confession. In that case, if it is possible to communicate by phone or by intercom from a distance away, the priest can offer consoling prayers and invite the person to offer prayers of perfect contrition and trust in God's mercy. The priest can offer appropriate prayers with family members and friends.

Anointing of the Sick

The sacrament of Anointing of the Sick not only is a sacrament of healing, but it carries with it the forgiveness of sins. That is why it can be administered only by a priest (c. 1003 §1) The sacrament should be administered, and even repeated consistent with canonical requirements, if requested by a person or his or her surrogate decision maker for an appropriate reason (e.g., danger due to sickness or old age). This applies for all people who have reached the age of reason, even if they are no longer able to exercise it. The canons speak to the administration of the sacrament in cases when the person "implicitly requested it" when he or she was competent (cc. 1004 §§1–2, 1005, 1006). However, the presumption that the person, if capable, would have asked for it—especially with grave illness or danger of death—could suffice. Before the penitent receives the sacrament, he or she must confess all serious sins that have not been confessed. If unable to do so, the penitent is to confess them as soon as possible, given the opportunity.

All priests entrusted with the care of souls have an obligation to administer this sacrament at the appropriate time (cc. 1001, 1003 §2). The sacrament is conferred by anointing with oil and pronouncing the words prescribed in the liturgical books (c. 998). "…In a case of necessity, however, a single anointing on the forehead or even on some other part of the body is sufficient, while the entire formula is said. The minister is to perform the anointings with his own hand, unless a grave reason warrants the use of an instrument" (c. 1000 §§1–2). Contagion presents a significant problem because of the proximity and physical contact between the priest and the person being anointed. This is not a sacrament administered at a distance. Also, the container of the oil of the sick cannot be brought into proximity of a patient nor reused between patients. The logistical hazards of contagion are very significant, and they affect not only the patient and the minister of the sacrament, but potentially everyone with whom he later has contact, and with all the individuals those persons later have contact.

The priest must follow strict protocol for entering and exiting the room, as directed by the health personnel. As stated earlier, it is also important to seek direction beforehand from the patient's health personnel about standards for not introducing pathogens into the patient's environment when bringing to the patient the Oil of the Sick. The use of oils and their receptables that have had direct or indirect contact with other persons must be prevented. There is the option for the priest to bless a very small amount of new Oil of the Sick (on the glove or swab) being used during that anointing: "In addition to a bishop, the following can bless the oil to be used in the anointing of the sick: ...any presbyter in a case of necessity, but only in the actual celebration of the sacrament" (c. 999, 2°).

Health care units should provide PPE for the priest, who can use an individual pre-oiled glove, or a long cotton-tipped swab (before the priest enters the patient's room; the container cannot enter the patient's room), or a similar item for anointing. Nothing that cannot be discarded in the patient room should be brought into the room. Formulas for any of the sacraments or blessings can be written on a disposable card (to be disposed of in the patient's room). The priest should review the procedure for hygienic purposes with facility personnel and follow it exactly (e.g., the swab or glove cannot be re-dipped in the holy oil). This would include the proper disposal of the glove and swab, which are single use. This can create a problem with liturgical law, requiring burning of the swab or glove due to remains of the Oil of the Sick. However, currently all patients are to be treated as if they have the COVID-19 virus. Removing from the room items, including instruments containing the holy oil, that have touched the patient or have touched other items in the room violates isolation precautions. Chaplains report discarding the swab and glove with the PPE in the patient's room. The priest can ask beforehand if the room contains a receptacle for biological waste, and if it is being burned, and if so, ask the staff to dispose of it there. Regardless, the instruments containing the holy oil are to be discarded in the patient's room. This clearly is less than ideal but herein one is dealing with what is possible.

Because of these significant hazards, it may be prudent to rely on general absolution or the Rite for Emergencies, addressed above, consistent with canon 960 and the directives of the diocesan bishop. Once the sacrament is administered and death is anticipated, the Apostolic pardon can be administered without proximity to the person.

Apostolic Pardon and Plenary Indulgence

An indulgence is the partial or plenary (total) remission of temporal punishment for sins already forgiven under certain conditions defined by the Church. All baptized members of the Christian faithful who are in communion with the

Church and in the state of grace may receive an indulgence. To gain a plenary indulgence, the person must have at least the general intention of acquiring it and must fulfill the three specific conditions: sacramental confession, Eucharistic communion, and prayer according to the Holy Father's intentions (cc. 992, 993, 996 §§1–2).

A great gift of the Church is the Apostolic pardon, a special plenary indulgence offered when death is imminent. The *Manual of Indulgences* states the following: "At the Point of Death a priest who administers the sacraments to someone in danger of death should not fail to impart the apostolic pardon to which a plenary indulgence is attached. If a priest is unavailable, Holy Mother Church benevolently grants to the Christian faithful, who are duly disposed, a plenary indulgence to be acquired at the point of death, provided they have been in the habit of reciting some prayers during their lifetime; in such a case, the Church supplies for the three conditions ordinarily required for a plenary indulgence."[13]

The Apostolic pardon is usually administered to a conscious or unconscious patient after the sacrament of Anointing of the Sick. It requires no direct contact with the recipient. Therefore, the diocesan bishop could consider approving the administration of the Apostolic pardon after the administration of individual absolution, after the Rite for Emergencies when integral confession or Anointing of the Sick are impossible, or when general absolution is administered, even using a bullhorn as cited above. A number of persons engaged in health care ministry, as well as the patients and families they serve, may be unaware of the Apostolic pardon. At the time of impending death, and in the absence of an available priest, the family or health care worker should help the patient to pray for such an indulgence, even if it is unclear whether the patient is conscious enough to do so. Again, our generous Church grants this plenary indulgence to persons who are properly disposed and who have been in the habit of reciting some prayers during their lifetime, as a substitute for the three usual conditions.[14]

A recent decree by the Apostolic Penitentiary on the granting of a plenary indulgence to the faithful in the current pandemic, expands on this further. The gift of special indulgences is granted to the faithful suffering from COVID-19 and their family members, as well as to health care workers who in any capacity care for them if with a spirit detached from any sin, they unite spiritually through the media to the celebration of Holy Mass, the recitation of the Holy Rosary, to the

---

[13] United States Conference of Catholic Bishops, *Manual of Indulgences* (Washington, DC: USCCB, 2006) n.12.

[14] Apostolic Penitentiary, "Note on the Sacrament of Reconciliation."

pious practice of the Way of the Cross or other forms of devotion, or if at least they will recite the Creed, the Lord's Prayer and a pious invocation to the Blessed Virgin Mary, offering this trial in a spirit of faith in God and charity towards their brothers and sisters, with the will to fulfil the usual conditions (sacramental confession, Eucharistic communion and prayer according to the Holy Father's intentions), as soon as possible.

Even those who pray for the end of the epidemic, relief for those who are afflicted, and eternal salvation for those who have died have access to the plenary indulgence under the same conditions if they "offer a visit to the Blessed Sacrament, or Eucharistic adoration, or reading the Holy Scriptures for at least half an hour, or the recitation of the Holy Rosary, or the pious exercise of the Way of the Cross, or the recitation of the Chaplet of Divine Mercy."[15]

Interestingly, when addressing the situation in which death is imminent and there is no access to the Anointing of the Sick or viaticum, the Apostolic Penitentiary states that the substitute for the three usual conditions for the plenary indulgence is having "recited a few prayers during their lifetime."[16] This demonstrates the pastoral care of the Church. For the attainment of this indulgence the use of the crucifix or the cross is recommended.[17]

Holy Eucharist/Viaticum

Reception of the holy Eucharist requires direct contact between the priest and recipient. One hears of "drive-by" opportunities, but this still requires close contact between minister and recipient. Furthermore, the delivery of the sacred host, even among a few recipients, requires serial touching of the sacred hosts. Again, it is important to seek direction beforehand from health personnel about standards for not introducing pathogens into the congregation or patient environments or transmitting pathogens from such environments. As cities, and churches within them, opened and liturgies and sacraments were again offered, dioceses developed safety protocols to protect the faithful and their ministers. However, the dying never should have been excluded from the sacraments, particularly the "last rites" of the Church. Unfortunately, there is growing evidence that they were. Critical to salvation at such a moment are sacraments that impart absolution: Anointing of the Sick and Penance, as addressed above.

---

[15] Apostolic Penitentiary, "Decree on Granting of Special Indulgences to the Faithful in the Current Pandemic" (March 20, 2020) https://press.vatican.va/content/salastampa/en/bollettino/pubblico/2020/03/20/200320c.html (accessed on 2 October 2020).

[16] Ibid.

[17] *Enchiridon indulgentiarum. Normae et concessiones* (Vatican City: Libreria Editrice Vaticana, 2009) n. 12.

While Holy Eucharist/Viaticum is a sacrament that imparts God's mercy and forgiveness, absolution of any grave sin is to precede it. Once imparted, if possible, the Holy Eucharist can be administered. However, great cautions need to be exercised to protect both minister and the faithful.

When bringing to the patient situation the Holy Eucharist, the priest must follow strict hygiene protocol for entering and exiting the room, as directed by the health personnel, including whatever PPE is required. Of course, at a minimum in all situations, protective mask and gloves are to be used. it is important to prevent the use of the host and pyx that have had contact with other persons. The pyx should not be opened in the patient room, nor brought into the patient room unless it remains secured under PPE. Nothing that cannot be discarded in the patient room should be brought into the room. Perhaps the host could be transferred to a clean disposable paper cup before entering the patient room. Also, it is important to ascertain if the patient can receive the host and if so, will the patient need it broken into a small piece, before entering the room. An unconsumed host creates a new set of hygienic procedures that would have to be addressed.

Additionally, there is evidence that some of the faithful are insisting on their right to only receive Holy Eucharist on the tongue, citing *Redemptionis sacramentum*, even when it imposes on the minister and others additional risks.[18] However, the dying patient may only be able to receive the Holy Eucharist on the tongue. Herein demonstrates the importance of protective equipment. Furthermore, prudence may dictate the use of the option, and great benefit, of a spiritual act of Holy Communion.

Providing Sacraments in Times of Pandemic

If there is ever a message to be received during this pandemic, it is the importance of the sacraments, not just because of their salvific nature, but also for the graces imparted by them. But access to grace abounds, for example, just praying for those affected by the pandemic, and fulfilling the related conditions, can affect a plenary indulgence.

There also is the tremendous need to minister to families of the victims of the pandemic. Required social isolation prevents family access to loved ones at the point of greatest need, when there is the danger of death. This is compounded by the reality that clergy may not have direct access to the dying, or even to their family members. Thankfully, technology enables the ministry to families to continue, even if through less ideal means.

---

[18]   Congregation for Divine Worship and Discipline of the Sacraments, Instruction *Redemptionis Sacramentum* 92 (25 March 2004).

During this pandemic, there are challenges in meeting the rights of the faithful to receive the sacraments. Such rights are circumscribed by specific conditions, including that sacraments be available at the appropriate time. The faithful are hungry for the sacraments, and there is great evidence that clergy are also suffered from their inability to provide them. They are seeking alternative ways to deliver them validly and safely. The responsibility of the diocesan bishop is significant: "Bishops are the principal dispensers of the mysteries of God, as well as being the governors, promoters, and guardians of the entire liturgical life in the church committed to them."[19] Thus, the diocesan bishop has great responsibility for assuring that the right to the sacraments is protected. There is the reality of the need to protect the faithful from a highly contagious disease that can be contracted through reception of the sacraments. However, sacraments critical to the salvation of souls as a person who is dying must remain available. Mechanisms to safely and validly provide them exist. However, the lack of direct sacramental access, especially to the dying, continues.

As cited above, one archdiocese has implemented the Apostolic Penitentiary's suggestion that priests collaborate with local health authorities to serve as "extraordinary hospital chaplains," complying with the norms of protection from contagion, "to guarantee the necessary spiritual assistance to the sick and dying."[20] This needs to become a national model. Furthermore, diocesan bishops and the United States Conference of Bishops must assert the right to the Church to exercise its ministries consistent with the First Amendment of the United States Constitution's Free Exercise [of religion] Clause.[21] It is understood that prudence dictates significant limitations on access to the sacraments. However, the faithful should never be denied the last rites of the Catholic Church, or at least sacramental absolution. There are ways to accomplish this safely, even it is through general absolution with a bullhorn.

Marie T. Hilliard, MS, MA, JCL, PhD, RN

---

[19] Second Vatican Council, *Christus Dominus*: Decree Concerning the Pastoral Office of Bishops in the Church 15 (Proclaimed by Pope Paul VI, October 28, 1965), citing Second Vatican Council, *Constitution on the Sacred Liturgy*, Dec. 4, 1963: *AAS* 56 (1964) 97 ff; Paul VI, *motu proprio Sacram Liturgiam*, Jan. 25, 1964: *AAS* 56 (1964) 139 ff; C. 835 §1: "The bishops in the first place exercise the sanctifying function; they are the high priests, the principal dispensers of the mysteries of God, and the directors, promoters, and guardians of the entire liturgical life in the church entrusted to them."
[20] Apostolic Penitentiary, Note on the Sacrament of Reconciliation.
[21] U.S. *Constitution*. amend I.

Canon 1247

Whether a Vigil Mass Can Fulfill Two Obligations

Sometimes a holy day of obligation (such as Christmas or the Immaculate Conception) falls on a Saturday or Monday. The Church allows us to fulfill our obligation to attend Mass for those days at a Mass the evening before the holy day or Sunday. Thus, the question frequently arises among the faithful: can attendance at one Mass on the evening of the Sunday, which is the evening before the holy day (or vice versa), fulfill the obligation for Sunday and the Holy Day?

Opinion

Yes, attendance at one Mass in the evening of a holy day of obligation that falls on Saturday fulfills the obligation.

The obligation to attend Mass on certain days arises from canon 1247: "On Sundays and other holy days of obligation, the faithful are obliged to participate in the Mass...". This obligation can, per canon 1248 §1, be fulfilled by attending a Mass the day of or even in the evening before: "A person who assists at a Mass celebrated anywhere in a Catholic rite either on the feast day itself or in the evening of the preceding day satisfies the obligation of participating in the Mass."

A plain text reading would seem to indicate that simply attending Mass on the evening of one feast which is also the evening before a Sunday (or vice versa) would suffice for both.

Some would say two obligations require two satisfactions.

Some canonists, however, hold that the canons impose an obligation for each Sunday and each holy day of obligation, and because those obligations are of the same type, they must be satisfied separately. Thus, for example, attending Mass on the evening of Saturday, December 8 cannot satisfy the obligations for both Sunday and the holy day. As one canonist sums up pithily: "Two Mass obligations require two Mass satisfactions. Period."[1]

---

[1] Edward Peters, "Two Mass obligations means two Masses, but...," in *In the Light of the Law: A Canon Lawyers Blog*, December 2, 2012, https://canonlawblog.wordpress.com /2012/12/02/two-mass-obligations-means-two-masses-but/ (accessed 27 September 2020).

But would that mean there are two obligations when a holy day falls on Sunday?

If there are two obligations that must be satisfied distinctly, however, then it would seem that when a holy day of obligation falls on a Sunday the faithful are obliged to attend Mass twice that day. If each holy day of obligation and Sunday impose a distinct obligation that cannot be fulfilled by one Mass, then how can one Mass satisfy two obligations when a holy day is on a Sunday? For example, in the year 2020 All Saints Day, a holy day of obligation, falls on Sunday, November 1. If "two Mass obligations require two Mass satisfactions" then it would seem that the faithful are obliged to attend Mass twice on November 1, 2020.

It might be thought that because the feast takes precedence over the Sunday, the obligation for the Sunday is suspended. However, the particular liturgy of the Mass is inconsequential to the question of fulfilling one's obligations. Just because it is the Solemnity of All Saints, it is also still Sunday.[2]

A non-obligatory solemnity or feast that trumps Sunday does not remove the obligation.

Furthermore, when a solemnity or feast that is a not a holy day of obligation liturgically trumps Sunday, are we then not required to participate in Mass on that Sunday? On Sunday, February 2, 2020 Catholics throughout the world celebrated the Feast of the Presentation of the Lord, which is not a holy day of obligation. Despite the fact that the non-obligatory Mass trumped the Sunday celebration, we were still obliged to attend Mass that day.[3]

Now, I am unaware of any canonist, theologian, or any arm-chair version of either who holds that if a holy day of obligation falls on a Sunday we are obliged to attend two Masses. But if we are not so required, can we really say that a vigil Mass that is in the evening of a holy day on a Saturday cannot fulfill both obligations?

---

[2] After all, when a Solemnity falls on a Friday (as All Saints Day did in 2019), it does not cease to be Friday, even though in such a case the Faithful are not obliged to abstain from meat (c. 1251).

[3] This is possibly the (perhaps unconscious) reason behind the strange situation that arises in the United States when December 8 is a Sunday. If December 8 is a Saturday or a Monday, it remains a holy day of obligation for Catholics in the United States because Our Blessed Mother is our patroness under that title. However, if December 8 falls on a Sunday, then the celebration of the solemnity is transferred to Monday, but the obligation is not transferred. Perhaps that is because the obligation was already fulfilled by Catholics who attended Mass on (Sunday) December 8.

The answer is that attendance at one Mass is sufficient.

I think the answer lies in returning to the plain text reading of the canon. We are obliged to attend Mass on Sundays and other holy days of obligation. We can fulfill this obligation either on the day itself or during the preceding evening. If we participate in a Mass during the preceding evening that also falls on a Sunday or holy day of obligation, then we observe two holy days with one Mass.

Rev. Samuel Spiering, JCL

CANON 1263

DIOCESAN TAXES

In addition to a parish assessment (tax), the diocesan bishop annually asks the faithful for contributions to a diocesan appeal for "charities and development." Each parish is assigned what is called a goal. If the parishioners' donations do not meet the goal, the balance is subsequently added to the previously established assessment and invoiced to the parish as "under goal" for the annual appeal. No promotional materials from the diocese mention that the parish will be billed for the "under goal" balance. Is the additional assessment valid? Must any canonical procedure be followed (e.g., c. 1263)? If so, must it be done each year? Alternatively, is this a penalty on the parish for failing to meet the goal? Can the bishop oblige the pastor to pay the "under goal" amount with monies given to the parish and not to the diocesan appeal?

OPINION

The Code of Canon Law treats four principal methods of raising revenue for the Church:

1) Fund raising drives or appeals or *subventions rogatae* (c. 1262): Fund raising drives or appeals are solicitations of funds made by official representatives of the Church, either inside or outside a church building, from a relatively large number of potential donors for more or less definite causes. These *subventiones rogatae* aim to making particular needs of the Church known to potential donors and appeal to their generosity. Although those conducting these fund-raising drives may set goals for the solicitation and even suggest specific donations, donors are free to contribute to the appeal as much or as little as they choose. Fundraising appeals are to be governed by norms enacted by the episcopal conference. The United States Conference of Catholic Bishops enacted such a norm in 2002 which was finally promulgated in 2007. This norm is the governing law for such fundraising at the moment.

2) Taxes or *tributa* or *exactiones* (c. 1263): Taxes (*tributa, exactiones*) are, as the word "exaction" suggests, compulsory defined monetary contributions imposed on persons, physical or juridic, or property by competent ecclesiastical authority for the purpose of supporting church

3) Fees or *taxa* and *oblationes* (c. 1264): *Taxae*, despite the similarity in sound to the English word "tax," are not taxes in the previously defined sense but fees expected for the performance of some administrative or ministerial services. Perhaps because of squeamishness about associating money with the administration of the sacraments and sacramental, the present law refers to so-called "stole fees" not as *taxae* as did the 1917 code but as offerings or *oblations*. The purpose of fees is not to fund church activities in general but to cover the costs of a particular service, much as the fee paid to the Department of Motor Vehicles for the renewal of a driver's license is not meant to fund local government but to cover the administrative costs of processing the application. Historically, the offerings or *oblations* tendered at the time of the administration of the sacraments or sacramentals were not designed to support the Church but to supplement the income of the minister. However, in the present law, these offerings are to be placed in a special parish account for a purpose designated by the diocesan bishop. (c. 531) In principle, payment of fees and offerings is obligatory. Nevertheless, ministers are cautioned not to so insist on *oblationes* for the administration of the sacraments and sacramentals that the poor would be deprived of them. (cc. 848 and 1181)

4) Collections or *stipes* or *oblations colligere* (c. 1266 and GIRM, §§73 and 140). Collections are free-will gifts or offerings made in the context of liturgical services. The Code mentions only special collections ordered by the local ordinary for some particular need, but the familiar "offertory collection" is treated in liturgical law. While the offertory collection is customary and taking up special collections in churches and oratories on days of precept can be mandated, contributing to these collections cannot be made compulsory. Indeed, the prohibition on charging for entry into churches at times of liturgical services has its origin in the efforts of the Holy See to extirpate the "door tax," a practice of charging a fee for entry into churches for the celebration of Mass which was common in many places in the United States well into the twentieth century.

Although fund raising appeals, taxes, fees and collections are distinct forms of raising revenue, they are often combined and sometimes confused. For example, special collections taken up in churches by order of the local ordinary are sometimes the vehicle chosen for carrying out a fundraising appeal. At other times, the form of a fund raising appeal is used to facilitate the collection of (or, perhaps, obscure the reality of) a tax, providing a spoonful of sugar to make the bitter medicine of a tax go down more easily. The critical distinction between a fundraising appeal or collection and a tax is that the latter is compulsory and the former is not.

The scenario described by the questioner seems to be a tax decked out in the language and trappings of a fundraising appeal. The diocesan bishop has determined to raise revenue for "charities and development" through solicitations made to the faithful of the diocese. In most such appeals with which I am familiar, while some of these solicitations may be made directly to previously identified potential donors by the bishop himself or the diocesan development office, the brunt of the solicitation is made at the parish level by the pastor. However, the diocese may provide promotional materials and strategies to assist in the solicitation. The bishop also sets a "goal" toward which the pastor should strive and may even provide incentives such as the ability to retain for parish projects some or all of the income in excess of the "goal." To this point, the solicitation appears to be a fundraising drive or *subventio rogata*. However, when the "goal" is a set amount whose payment is compulsory whether or not it is covered by free will offerings from the faithful, the "goal" has become a tax even if thinly disguised as a fundraising appeal.

The 1983 Code of Canon Law authorizes the diocesan bishop to levy "a moderate tax for the needs of the diocese upon public juridic persons subject to his governance." (c. 1263) In practice, these public juridic persons subject to the diocesan bishop's governance will be parishes. This tax can only be based on income. Before levying the tax, the diocesan bishop must first consult both the diocesan finance council and the presbyteral council. Although the diocesan bishop is not bound to follow the advice these bodies give him, failure to consult them renders the act of imposing invalid. (c. 127, §1) In the case presented by the questioner, the mandatory "goal" or tax for charities and development would be valid if the so-called "goal" was determined as a proportion of the income of the parishes taxed and if the diocesan finance council and presbyteral council had been consulted prior to its enactment. If the tax was validly levied, the pastor is bound to pay it from general parish income. Payment of the tax is not a penalty but simply one of the "costs of doing business" like paying the electric bill and insurance premiums. If, however, the so-called "goal" is not based on parish income or was not enacted pursuant to the required consultations, the tax is invalid and not binding on the parish or the pastor. Efforts by the bishop to collect an invalid tax or to discipline the pastor for failure to remit the "underage" would exceed the bishop's authority.

There is not unanimity among the canonical commentators about whether new consultations are required each year a tax is collected if it is an ongoing exaction. In most governmental systems, taxation is an act of legislative power. This would seem to be true in the Church as well. The power to impose *tributa* and *exactiones* is reserved to the diocesan bishop (cc. 1263 and 264) who alone possesses legislative power in the diocese. When Congress enacts an income tax scheme, it is a law which remains in force year after year until Congress terminates or alters it. The amount individuals pay in tax each year may vary as their income varies but the law itself has not changed. In the opinion of this canonist, the same is true of church taxes. When, after due consultation, the diocesan bishop levies a tax on parish income that is intended to continue from year to year, no new consultations are required in subsequent years as long as the tax scheme remains unaltered. The tax scheme may be progressive so that more affluent parishes pay a higher percentage of their income than do poorer parishes; it may limit taxable income to "ordinary revenues," exempt certain forms of income (e.g., bequests in wills) from taxations, and give credit for certain expenditures (e.g., subsidies to parish schools). However, if the tax scheme is to be changed (e.g., by changing the percentages for calculating tax liability or the income covered by the tax) new consultations with the diocesan finance council and presbyteral council are required for the validity of the tax.

Reverend John P. Beal, III

CANON 1447 AND *DIGNITAS CONNUBII* ART. 36 AND 66

FROM JUDGE TO DEFENDER OF THE BOND IN THE SAME CAUSE?

At a first instance tribunal, the judicial vicar establishes a collegiate tribunal for a specific case to declare a marriage null by means of the ordinary process. One of the judges was then replaced by the judicial vicar and appointed ad hoc Defender of the Bond, another person was appointed third judge for the collegiate tribunal. Does this rise to the level of admitting a complaint of nullity of sentence?

OPINION

The Law

Before commenting on this scenario, one has to recall canon 18 which states: "Laws which establish a penalty, restrict the free exercise of rights, or contain an exception from the law are subject to strict interpretation."

Canon 1447 reads: "A person who has taken part in a case as a judge, promoter of justice, defender of the bond, procurator, advocate, witness, or expert cannot later in another instance validly decide the same case as judge or perform the function of assessor."

In a similar fashion the instruction *Dignitas connubii* states in article 66 § 1: "One who has taken part in a cause as a judge cannot afterwards in another instance validly decide the same cause as a judge or carry out the function of assessor (cf. can. 1447)."

Following the norm of canon 18, it means that anyone appointed as a judge in a previous instance, cannot act as a judge or assessor in another instance in the same cause. The focus of the scenario is not on the question whether or not someone can exercise functions in a stable manner at tribunals that are connected by reason of appeal according to *Dignitas connubii* article 36 § 1, but on the question if a person initially appointed judge of a collegiate tribunal can function as defender of the bond in the same cause in the same instance. Canon 1447 and *Dignitas connubii* article 66 § 1 refer to the impossibility to be a judge in the first and its appeal instance. Canon 1447 and *Dignitas connubii* article 66 § 1 do not provide an answer to the problem raised in the aforementioned scenario, the possibility to initially be appointed judge of a collegiate tribunal and then as defender of the bond in the same instance in the same cause.

150

Dignitas connubii article 66 § 2 states: "One who has taken part in a cause as a defender of the bond, promoter of justice, procurator, advocate, witness or expert cannot in the same or another instance validly decide the same cause as a judge or carry out the function of assessor (cf. can. 1447)."

This norm may appear to give an answer to the question posed. Once appointed defender of the bond, one cannot in the same instance decide the same cause as a judge. Referring back to canon 18, strict interpretation, it means, article 66 § 2 speaks of the situation that someone was initially appointed defender of the bond, then removed as defender of the bond and appointed as judge (whether sole judge or a judge of a collegiate tribunal) in the same cause. The reason for this impossibility is that a defender of the bond is considered a party[1] of the case with a special interest: to defend the marriage bond. Therefore, anyone appointed initially as defender of the bond can be considered biased and cannot exercise later the function as ecclesiastical judge. The case scenario is the opposite: someone appointed initially judge of a collegiate tribunal is later called to function as defender of the bond.

Dignitas connubii article 36 § 2 states: "The same officials are not to exercise simultaneously two functions in a stable manner in the same tribunal, without prejudice to art. 53, § 3." This means, that someone cannot be appointed judge and defender of the bond in a stable manner at the same tribunal. This norm appears to refer to the case scenario but the clause "in a stable manner" does not apply. The judge was appointed *ad hoc* defender of the bond; the judge was not appointed defender of the bond in a stable manner at the tribunal. Therefore, the norm itself does not apply: the person had only one stable function at the tribunal, and article 36 § 2 makes no reference to the impossibility in the same cause.

Lüdicke/Jenkins' provides the following comment on *Dignitas connubii* article 36: "Appointment to one of the functions in individual cases is possible so long as the functions are not fulfilled in the same cause."[2] This statement is clear concerning the effects on a case in which someone fulfills two functions that the person shouldn't have. The following may be taken into consideration: The commentary does not include the clause that the appointment to the function is to

---

[1] Although commonly one refers to the petitioner and the respondent as party of a case, the defender of the bond is a party as well. While the petitioner and maybe also the respondent intend to have their marriage declared null, the assumed valid marriage bond itself needs to be protected and represented; this is done by the defender of the bond. Furthermore, interpreting canon 1514, the defender of the bond is referred to directly in this norm as a party of the case.

[2] K. LÜDICKE and R. JENKINS, *Dignitas Connubii. Norms and Commentary* (Alexandria, VA: Canon Law Society of America, 2006) 82.

be "in a stable manner." Could it leave the possibility that someone might have been appointed judge of a collegiate tribunal to a case and was later exercising the function as defender of the bond after being appointed *ad hoc* defender of the bond? Lüdicke/Jenkins refer in the commentary to exercising, "fulfilling" two incompatible functions, and "the appointment to one of the functions."

Indeed, the judge was initially appointed judge to a cause, but does the appointment itself rise to the level of "fulfilling" the function at the time of appointment? If the person was appointed *praeses* of the case, then he could not be validly acting as defender of the bond; the next judicial step after the formulation of doubt is the order for the instruction of the case, which is done by the presiding judge. If the judge was not the *praeses*, could that judge, after being replaced, function as defender of bond? A consideration could be, to question if the judge originally named did nothing pending the outcome of the inquiry and had no knowledge of the cause or, was the judge directly involved in the case. If the judge was involved, he certainly cannot be a defender of the bond in the same case, i.e. was involved in the instruction of the case or after the conclusion of the case. But, if it were just an appointment - pro forma - at the beginning, and he knew nothing about the case, then - maybe - it was illicit probably, but not necessarily invalid? The reason: he was not "fulfilling" his function as judge as he only received a notice of appointment to the case and a notice that he was replaced as judge, but had no access to the file itself, and as defender of the bond, he was "fulfilling" his function, i.e. having access to the case, be part of the instruction of the case, preparing the observations as defender of the bond, etc.

Since the law and the instruction do not directly refer to such a case, and commentaries rather rely on "exercising" or "fulfilling" a certain function, it may allow for the possibility in case of a collegiate tribunal if several above mentioned conditions are fulfilled; as sole judge it is definitively not possible since the sole judge had knowledge of the case soon after the constitution of tribunal if the sole judge himself is not the judicial vicar; in case he is the judicial vicar, he had knowledge of the case from the moment of receiving and accepting the petition.

Prof. Michael Nobel, PhD, JCL

Canons 1483, 1484

Whether the *Ex Officio* Appointment of a Procurator-Advocate Is Subject to Diocesan Limitations

A judicial vicar has legitimately cited the respondent of a case who indicated that he does not want to participate in the proceedings. To safeguard the right of defense, the judicial vicar appoints ex officio *a procurator-advocate for the respondent. Although the local tribunal of diocese X has a list of procurator-advocates, the judicial vicar, having determined that a specific person is more suitable for the case at hand, appoints someone from diocese Y as the respondent's procurator-advocate.*

Opinion

It is common practice at local tribunals for a judicial vicar or *praeses*, depending on the stage of the process, to appoint *ex officio* a procurator-advocate from a list of already approved procurator-advocates, if a party does not want to appoint a procurator-advocate but the judge finds the service of a procurator-advocate necessary. A procurator-advocate may be appointed for a respondent who does not want to participate in the process itself and either

a) refuses to testify and to appoint a procurator-advocate, but is not declared absent, or

b) is declared absent because the respondent

   i) does not want to testify and participate in any way nor to communicate or to be contacted by the tribunal itself, or

   ii) has whereabouts that are truly unknown.

The requirements to be considered procurator and/or advocate are outlined in canon 1483: "The procurator and advocate must have attained the age of majority and be of good reputation; moreover, the advocate must be a Catholic unless the diocesan bishop permits otherwise, a doctor in canon law or otherwise truly expert, and approved by the same bishop." Stricter requirements, at least the approval by the diocesan bishop, apply for an advocate, but to exercise this function is ultimately the discretion of the diocesan bishop. For example, he can determine whether the advocate has to be a Catholic or has to have a doctorate in canon law or a canonical degree at all.

According to canon 1484 §1: "Before the procurator and advocate undertake their function, they must present an authentic mandate to the tribunal." When the judicial vicar or *praeses* appoints a procurator-advocate *ex officio*, this mandate is given through the decree of appointment itself, and it must be signed by the appointee. One question remains: Who can be chosen as procurator-advocate in a case? Common practice is the appointment of those already approved by the bishop moderator for this function in a specific diocese. Is a judicial vicar or *praeses* bound by this list? Does a procurator-advocate whose name is on the list have to have a diocesan domicile according to canon 102 to be eligible for consideration and approval by the bishop moderator, and, consequently, is there a limitation to diocesan jurisdiction?

As seen in canon 1483, there is no requirement for a procurator-advocate to have a diocesan domicile to be capable to exercise the function of procurator and/or advocate at any local tribunal. The only limitation in the case of an advocate is the approval of the bishop moderator. Therefore, those who fulfill the requirements as per canon 1483 and independent of their domicile can be approved by a bishop moderator; and their names can be placed on a local tribunal's list of procurator-advocates. One can interpret this as a "pre-screening and approval" so that the parties of a case and the judicial vicar/*praeses* can have immediate access to available personnel, especially in the case of an advocate.

There are two other options available to a judicial vicar/*praeses* that are not often utilized:

1) A judicial vicar/*praeses* can appoint *ad casum* a procurator-advocate from another local tribunal's list. The law does not indicate that he would need a specific reason to do so, nor that he is bound by the local list of his own tribunal. Nevertheless, he would still require the approval from his bishop moderator due to the stricter limitations for an advocate. One may argue whether or not the approval of his bishop moderator is necessary, since the bishop moderator of the other tribunal already verified that this person fulfills all canonical requirements to be appointed advocate.

2) A judicial vicar/*praeses* can appoint *ad casum* a procurator-advocate who is not on any local tribunal's list. As long as the selected person fulfills the requirements as per canon 1483, a judicial vicar/*praeses* can appoint this person as procurator-advocate for a specific case. Nevertheless, he would still require the approval from his bishop moderator due to the stricter limitations for an advocate.

In both cases, and to avoid any injustice of the process and the sentence, e.g. canon 1620, 6° and/or 7°, canon 18 ("Laws which establish a penalty, restrict the free exercise of rights, or contain an exception from the law are subject to strict interpretation.") must be applied and a brief notification should be sent to the bishop moderator seeking his approval for the *ad casum* proposed procurator-advocate. In the first case, the judicial vicar/*praeses* can state that this person is already approved for this function in another diocese, and in the latter case, he would have to give more detailed information so that the bishop moderator can approve the proposed *ad casum* for this function at his local tribunal.

Prof. Michael Nobel, PhD, JCL

Canon 1673 §§ 3 and 4

Whether a Judicial Vicar Can Appoint a Sole Judge in Cases of Nullity of Marriage

A judicial vicar has established the formulation of doubt, and in the same decree, admits a case to the ordinary process and appoints a sole judge.

Opinion

It is common practice at local tribunals for a judicial vicar to appoint a sole judge in cases of nullity of marriage, oftentimes without two assessors. Prior to outline the requirements of canon 1673 §§ 3 and 4, one has to recall canon 18: "Laws which establish a penalty, restrict the free exercise of rights, or contain an exception from the law are subject to strict interpretation." The point of reference of canon 18 is the restriction of the free exercise of rights that a judicial vicar may or may not enjoy.

Canon 1673 §3 states that "cases of nullity of marriage are reserved to a college of three judges. A judge who is a cleric must preside over the college, but the other judges may be laypersons." This prescript is similar to canon 1425 §1, 1°: "With every contrary custom reprobated, the following cases are reserved to a collegiate tribunal of three judges: 1° ... b) concerning the bond of marriage ..." Therefore, the judicial vicar has the right to establish a collegiate tribunal, which is also stated in canon 1676 §3: "If the case is to be handled through the ordinary process, the judicial vicar ... is to arrange the constitution of a college of judges."

The term *disponat*, translated "to arrange," is to be understood in this context as the competency of the judicial vicar "to establish" a collegiate tribunal. If he does so, the rule of law is observed and the process can be handled by the number of judges prescribed by law – it would not result in remediable nullity according to canon 1622, 1°: "A sentence suffers from the defect of remediable nullity only if: it was rendered by an illegitimate number of judges contrary to the prescript of can. 1425 §1."

Questions arise on the interpretation of the term "to arrange" in canon 1676 §3 with regards to the appointment of a sole judge. Indeed, canon 1676 §3 states: "If the case is to be handled through the ordinary process, the judicial vicar ... is to arrange the constitution of a college of judges or of a single judge with two assessors according to can. 1673 §4." This reference canon, however, gives the competency to entrust a case to a sole judge to the bishop moderator, not the judicial vicar: "The bishop moderator, if a collegial tribunal cannot be constituted in the diocese or in a nearby tribunal chosen according to the norm of §2, is to entrust cases to a sole clerical judge who, where possible, is to employ two assessors … unless it is otherwise evident, the same single judge has competency for those things attributed to the college, the *praeses*, or the *ponens*." According to article 24, §2 *Dignitas connubii*, the "bishop moderator is understood to be the diocesan bishop in regard to a diocesan tribunal."

This prescript of canon 1673 §4 is similar to canon 1425 §4: "If it happens that a collegiate tribunal cannot be established in the first instance of a trial, the conference of bishops can permit the bishop, for as long as the impossibility continues, to entrust cases to a single clerical judge who is to employ an assessor and auditor where possible" (similar article 30, §3 *Dignitas connubii*) The *mens legislatoris* in cases of sole judges, whether in cases of nullity of marriage or in any ordinary contentious trial, is the same: the appointment is done by the bishop (with a further condition [necessary permission from the conference of bishops] for ordinary contentious trials). By law, the judicial vicar cannot appoint a sole clerical judge for cases of nullity of marriage; he can either appoint a collegiate tribunal, or he can substitute judges, sole judges included, according to canon 1425 §5.

Therefore, how is the term *disponat* to be understood in the context of canon 1676 §3? If a collegial tribunal cannot be established, "to arrange" appears to mean "to inform" the bishop moderator who, according to canon 1673 §4, can appoint a sole clerical judge, not the judicial vicar; therefore, "to arrange" in the context of a sole judge means to make arrangements that the bishop can and does appoint a sole judge if a collegial tribunal cannot be established.

An important question arises based on this information: Does a judicial sentence rendered by a sole judge, appointed by the judicial vicar, suffer from a defect of nullity? It is not subject to canon 1620 on irremediable nullity, since a sole judge is not an incompetent judge. Furthermore, canon 1620 does not refer to a judicial vicar appointing a sole judge. Could it be subject to canon 1622, 1°, that "it was rendered by an illegitimate number of judges," since the law ascribes competency to the judicial vicar to only appoint a college of judges, but reserves the appointment of a sole judge to the bishop if a collegiate tribunal cannot be established? If so, the sentence would suffer from remediable nullity. With reference to canon 1623, if the sentence is not challenged within three months from the notice of its publication by the parties of the case and/or the defender of the bond, the sentence is valid and stands.

157

Canon 18 requires strict interpretation, and an important condition stated in canon 1673 §4 is the impossibility to establish a collegiate tribunal. What if a collegiate tribunal could be established but the judicial vicar appoints only a sole clerical judge? One could argue that it falls in the same category as above, and canon 1622, 1° would apply, since marriage cases are to be handled with by a collegiate tribunal – it is important to understand the distinction: handled through the ordinary process by a collegiate tribunal is not "adjudicated by a collegiate tribunal." Canon 1676 does not speak of "adjudication," which would refer only to the sentencing part of the process and would falsely permit initially the appointment of a sole judge for the instructional phase.

Could the judicial vicar defer to canon 1424: "In any trial, a single judge can employ two assessors who consult with him; they are to be clerics or lay persons of upright life." The answer is: no. This norm does not refer to a) who can appoint the sole judge, and b) one cannot read the norm independent from its context (see canon 17), since canon 1425 ascribes competency to appoint a sole judge to the bishop only; for marriage cases this is specifically stated in canon 1673 §4.

In conclusion: by law itself, the judicial vicar cannot appoint a sole judge for cases of nullity of marriage; he can appoint a collegiate tribunal or substitute judges. If he appoints a sole judge and the sentence is not challenged within three months, the sentence is valid.

Proposal: to avoid unnecessary delays with regards to "to arrange" for the appointment of a sole judge by the bishop moderator according to canon 1673 §4, or the possibility of challenging the sentence according to canon 1622, the diocesan bishop could delegate the appointment of a sole judge to the judicial vicar. As Beal states: "There are, however, some routine 'housekeeping' tasks that the law reserves to the diocesan bishop that could be usefully delegated to the judicial vicar. These include: 1) Entrusting marriage cases to a single clerical judge ... Without compromising the bishop's oversight of the work of the tribunal, delegation of these rather mundane and frequently recurring tasks to the judicial vicar can prevent the needless delays in the process that can result when the tribunal must wait until the bishop is available to entertain and approve these requests."[1] The judicial vicar, who does not enjoy the faculty by law, can act due to delegation. Beal's proposal seems acceptable although he does not offer a legal foundation for the delegation "of these rather mundane and frequently recurring tasks." Beal's proposal is partially in the spirit of canon 134 §3, although this canon only refers to delegating the vicar general and episcopal vicars. In addition,

---

[1] John P. Beal, "*Mitis Iudex* Canons 1671-1682, 1688-1691: A Commentary," in *The Jurist*, 75 (2015) 477-478.

according to Beal's proposal, the delegation could be exercised, according to canon 1673 §4, only if a collegiate tribunal cannot be established. Would it be a valid exercise of delegation if the judicial vicar simply appoints a sole judge for financial and time related reasons, although he could appoint a collegiate tribunal? And, what is the "objective" criterion that a collegiate tribunal cannot be established? The law permits one's own diocesan judges, the assistance from the neighboring tribunal, *ad hoc* appointment of judges from other dioceses, etc. As indicated above, it could rise to the level of remediable nullity, and, if not challenged, the sentence would be valid once three months after the notification of the sentence have passed.

Prof. Michael Nobel, PhD, JCL

SST Article 6, §1, 2°

Temporary Possession in Penal Law

What constitutes "temporary" possession of illicit images, as indicated in the recent Vademecum from the Congregation for the Doctrine of the Faith?

Opinion

Sacramentorum sanctitatis tutela article 6, §1, 2° described as a delict, "the acquisition, possession, or distribution by a cleric of pornographic images of minors [...] for purposes of sexual gratification, by whatever means or using whatever technology." In a *vademecum* issued by the Congregation for the Doctrine of the Faith on 16 July 2020 we find a new adjectival phrase modifying the word "possession." Section 1, № 6 of the *vademecum* reads: "the acquisition, possession (even temporary) or distribution by a cleric of pornographic images of minors." It will be important for canonists investigating accusations of this delict to know how computers function and what proofs establish "temporary" possession of illicit material. Proof of possession should include some account of the intention to acquire the material.

Internet browsing and caches

Cases involving this delict are likely to concern material transmitted over the Internet. An image file that someone saves onto his computer's hard drive for easy and convenient access is something he can be said to possess, and the act of saving the file indicates his intention to retain the image. Images viewed on a website but not permanently saved call for a more nuanced analysis.

A computer (or smart phone or similar device) does not function like a telescope, giving the user a view of an object located somewhere far away. Rather, a computer functions more like a fax machine: when a user desires to view a web page, document, image, or file, the user's computer asks for this object from the far-away computer or server on which it is located. The server (contacted via the Internet) then sends that document, image, or file to the user's computer. Like in the fax machine analogy, there now exist two identical copies of the original image: one on the server of the website in question, and a brand-new copy located on the user's computer.

Additionally, it is important to know that images obtained from the Internet are usually stored long-term on a computer, in what is called a *cache*. Mark

Nottingham, a member of the Internet Architecture Board, explains that a cache: "lets you set aside a section of your computer's hard disk to store representations that you've seen." Storing copies of images on a local computer reduces loading time when visiting websites, which allows a re-visited page (such as when pressing the 'back' button in a web browser) to be "served from browsers' caches almost instantaneously."[1] Unless a person using a computer takes special precautions to prevent the long-term storage of Internet images, any picture seen on the Internet will continue to exist on that person's computer for some time, even if the computer is turned off and on again. It is, however, possible to manually delete these images from a computer.

Given this description of how a computer functions, one could say that anyone whose computer has displayed an image from the Internet "possessed" a copy of that image, inasmuch as it did exist on the user's computer, at least temporarily. But an overly literal interpretation of possession is not sufficient to establish delictual behavior.

Jurisprudence

On 24 March 2017, officials from the Congregation for the Doctrine of the Faith visited The Catholic University of America in Washington, D.C., to offer a workshop for canonists, entitled: "The More Grave Delicts – Jurisprudence and Practice." In a program on the subject of *Sacramentorum sanctitatis tutela* articles 4 and 6, it was noted regarding the delict in question that downloading pornographic images of minors is a choice, an activity that requires specific selection of this precise kind of material. Such images—illegal in almost all civil jurisdictions worldwide—often can be accessed only after paying fees, sometimes requiring special programs or apps. The simple fact that this material exists on someone's computer usually demonstrates intentionality.

That having been said, it was stated that the *praxis curiae* of the Congregation was to require that intentionality must be established in order to constitute delictual "possession." Possession was described as keeping the images available by maintaining them in a virtual or real place where they can be accessed. A computer's browsing history (a record that a certain website was visited on a certain date) is relevant to a criminal investigation but does not prove intention nor establish possession. Similarly, a "bookmark" or stored link to an offending website might not, by itself, serve as proof of a conscious and voluntary retention

---

1 Mark Nottingham, "Caching Tutorial for Web Authors and Webmasters," https://www.mnot.net/cache_docs/ (accessed 23 July 2020).

of prohibited material. These facts generally do not prove possession, properly understood. No existing jurisprudence establishes mere viewing as possession, despite what one might argue from a literal explanation of how a browser cache actually functions. Locating these images as actually still extant in a computer's cache, however, might be sufficient to prove "possession" as this term is understood by the Congregation for the Doctrine of the Faith.

Conclusion and implications beyond SST

Although the CDF indicates that "even temporary" possession is sufficient possession for the purposes of the delict concerning pornographic images of minors described in SST, delictual "possession" should not be understood as including the fleeting digital copies of material that result from an instantaneous or accidental visit to an offending website. However, in cases of not only immoral but delictual material, it is usually possible to establish intentionality from the circumstances that surround the way in which the images were obtained. I would further suggest that this standard of possession might inform, not only cases of grave delicts, but also interventions concerning non-delictual behavior involving illicit images that are not illegal in civil law. Diocesan human resources policies or clergy handbooks may outline specific consequences for "possession" of pornographic material acquired using diocesan or parish computer equipment. If such an investigation is ever undertaken, the standards of possession as understood by the Congregation for the Doctrine of the Faith should be looked to as the rule for establishing possession of similar kinds of illicit material, even when this material does not involve a grave delict.

Rev. Peter B. Mottola, BS (Information Technology), JCL

CONTRIBUTORS

Rev. Brian T. Austin, FSSP, JCD, PhD, has experience at the Metropolitan Tribunal of Miami, FL.

Rev. John P. Beal, III is a priest of the Diocese of Erie and a professor of canon law at the Catholic University of America in Washington, DC.

Very Rev. Patrick Cooney, OSB, JCL, is the Judicial Vicar for the Diocese of Owensboro, Kentucky.

Rev. Msgr. Brendan P. Daly, JCD, is Judicial Vicar for the Tribunal of the Catholic Church in New Zealand and a lecturer in canon law at Good Shepherd College.

Dr. Marie T. Hilliard, MS, MA, JCL, PhD, RN, is a Senior Fellow Ethicist at the National Catholic Bioethics Center.

Dr. Eileen C. Jaramillo, DMin, JCL, is a Professor of Canon Law at Siena Heights University in Adrian, Michigan, and a Canonical Consultant in Lansing, Michigan.

Rev. Msgr. Charles M. Mangan, JCL, is the Vicar for Consecrated Life for the Diocese of Sioux Falls, South Dakota.

Sr. Rose McDermott, SSJ, is a retired professor of canon law and is the Delegate for Religious for the Diocese of Trenton.

Mrs. Donna Miller, JD, JCL, is the Executive Coordinator for the Canon Law Society of America residing in The Villages, FL.

Rev. Peter B. Mottola, B.S. (Information Technology), JCL, is a priest of the Diocese of Rochester with chancery experience and a degree in Medieval Studies.

Prof. Michael Nobel, PhD, JCL is a professor of canon law at the University of St.Paul in Ottawa, Ontario, Canada.

Very Rev. Kenneth A. Riley, JCL, has served as Vicar General, Chancellor and Judicial Vicar for the Diocese of Kansas City - St. Joseph in Missouri.

Rev. Msgr. Michael A. Souckar, JCD, is the Adjutant Judicial Vicar for the Archdiocese of Miami, Florida, and Pastor of St. Andrew Catholic Church in Coral Springs, Florida.

Rev. Samuel Spiering, JCL, is a priest of the Diocese of Great Falls – Billings, Montana, and he is pastor of Saint Leo the Great Catholic Parish.

Made in the USA
Monee, IL
25 October 2020

46024091R00095